LOOK @ the L

Modern Shopping

By

Jennifer Countess von Walderdorff

Table of Contents

Dedication

This book is dedicated first and foremost to my parents, who were born with the most unique, natural style which, by the miracles of hereditary biology, was inherited to me. I also dedicate this book to my brother Henry, a man of practicality, whom I particularly love shopping for, despite the incredibly practical gifts he dispenses to me. My sister Rebecca, an absolute genius copywriter and wordsmith, and Josephine, who always looked out for me as a big sister, despite the mere one-year age gap. Thanks to you all; you helped create this.

I also dedicate this book to the consumer, to you and me. To anyone who has ever been shafted, fleeced, or misled when paying for a beloved item. Maybe even straying slightly beyond the month's budget on a coat, bag, shoes or outfit, only to find out it's a synthetic, dry-clean only, expensive-for-nothing piece of cloth that wasn't worth the oil it was synthesised from. Relax that British stiff upper lip, and go get your refund (unworn, with receipt, of course – I don't want to start a riot). Pay for the quality you deserve, with style built in by manufacturers with the foresight to think of the future.

Acknowledgement

The completion of this book could not have been possible without the encouragement and assistance of so many people, whose names may not be stated but many of which are related to me by blood. I greatly value and appreciate their help and reassurance. I would like express a special acknowledgment to Ada, Henry, Elizabeth, Andrew, Josephine and Rebecca, my siblings, who without their love and support this book would not be possible. As well as my one in a million mum Agnes, who encouraged my free thinking and mould breaking. Additionally, my husband, for falling in love with a head-strong, eccentric woman and supporting me throughout the construction of this book.

About the Author

Jennifer was born and raised in London, England by her Nigerian parents. Along with her 6 siblings, she was raised Catholic, and lived a full life. She initially had her sights set on being a doctor, but a twist of fate allowed Jennifer, with her mother's blessing, to pursue her love of maths and fashion. She went into a career in fashion merchandising and even started her own accessories company, Cheeky Poppins. After spending over 15 years in the fashion retail industry, leading departments for both retailer and own-brand teams, she picked up more than a few nuggets of wisdom. Having worked for some of the most influential brands and retailers, she saw a common gap in the average consumer's knowledge. Jennifer not only wanted to fill that space with education, she also wanted to encourage us all to shop smarter. To stop limiting ourselves to certain brands, sizes or fabrics – and to explore all the options and find what works best, both economically and aesthetically, for us personally. Most recently, working for the largest online retailer in Europe (Zalando), planning the supply for hundreds of brands – this has enabled Jennifer to acquire an overview few get to see, both analytically and strategically, for the future growth of a successful company.

Jennifer refers to herself as a hard worker, with "prepare to fail if you fail to prepare" as one of her personal mantras. She didn't see it coming when the love of her life fell into her lap so easily, weeks after emigrating to Germany. But here she is, a real multi-hyphenate: Countess, wife, mother, analyst, author and entrepreneur, ready to conquer the world.

Foreword

Benjamin Krummel, CPO International Deichmann

We all enjoy fashion, whether from a professional, personal, craft or aesthetic standpoint. On top of this, fashion builds economies and can help them recover from depression. I have been working in the fashion industry for years, and as a CPO I have seen a sea of brands come in and out like the tide. There are, of course, those that remain as static as the sun. The variety on the market now is possibly the widest it has ever been, with no sign of narrowing again any time soon. It is therefore refreshing to witness a bright young star produce a witty and informative book about fashion, how to shop, what to look for, and how to make the brands work for you. Jennifer breaks down stereotypes, making words like *affordable* no longer sound ugly. Fast fashion is growing quickly, so keeping an eye on that which fills our wardrobes should be encouraged. This book speaks to people without selling, this book has a voice, this book has opinions, many of which I share.

Introduction

I am Jennifer, and I am a fashion business owner, writer, merchandiser, business strategist, and analyst. I'm also an all-round anal-retentive woman with a huge enthusiasm for bravura and style. Being a bit of a geek-freak for the fashion industry, I have worked in multiple departments throughout my merchandising career leading strategic planning teams in Europe and the USA. My hands-on school of fashion, which amalgamated into a business, and my writing vocation came as a surprise to some, given that I graduated with a 2:1 Bachelor of Science degree in Medical Biology!

With my analytical approach I've examined data in reference to fashion categories, terms, definitions, and general strategies concerning what to buy, sell, and invest in. Many of these questions are asked by those who do not have years of experience in fashion retail, or even an interest beyond what looks good on them and what they can afford each month. I took the ubiquity of many terms for granted, until I was asked questions like, 'What is "A-line", Jen?', and 'What does this symbol mean on the bottom of the shoe?' Questions which when answered, were often met with disbelief. The best one was a text from a male friend: 'Jen, if anyone will know you will – what the hell is viscose, buying a dress for my sister.' My reply came quick, hoping to spare his sister, who had just given birth. 'Run away, fast, and pretend you didn't see it.' Viscose does have a time and a place, in my opinion, and it is fast fashion for those with no use for it after its initial wear. More on this topic later.

I'm affectionately known by my friends and family as a style coach. I have assisted with styling on international fashion shows, and run a novel bespoke fashion-accessory business as the primary stakeholder. In my spare time, I am literally and figuratively running in heels (platforms) as the researcher and resource centre on the fashion industry for friends and family. For context, I have six siblings, five siblings-in-law and six nieces and nephews, plus my mum and a bunch of lunatics who refer to me as their friend. Thinking in the scope of my day job, I believe it is mandatory to understand the requirements of all different shapes, tastes, and ages, as well as the sprogs – kids have their own identity if you let them create it (otherwise you run the risk of creating a 'mini-me').

I try to deliver life skills, the equivalent of learning how to start a fire if stranded on a desert island. Life throws curveballs: weight gain and loss, new jobs, change of location and climate, all sorts. Adapting to each will be so much easier if you have a guide such as this to help you shop for what you require, topping up your knowledge to get exactly what you want, complemented with that information you need.

In this guide or within the handy appendix at the back you will find titbits of information about fabrics, styles, lengths – the difference between twill and jersey, A-line or bubble, mini or midi lengths. This stuff will not only clue you up to streamline your shopping, but could also help you save a fortune, and to only buy what you are really after. I don't judge an avid shopper – after all, I am one! – and I'm not trying to slow you down, either; I just want to breathe some life into the process to help you see what you may not have noticed before. I have deposits of clothes and accessories all over my home, a shopaholic's hidden wardrobe. I have winter and summer storage in my mother's cellar at the family home in London, including more than five suitcases of accessories, footwear, outerwear and beachwear. Fashions which will probably come back around in another five years or so (every two years for flares). In my current home in Berlin, I store the counter-seasonal fashion away under the bed, in the wardrobe and the closet. The way I figure it, there's no point taking up space with weather-inappropriate attire when I can accommodate the things I need on a daily basis.

My living space is built up with hat boxes, bag shelving and scarf dividers, plus the shoe racks and coat hangers; but I wouldn't trade it for the world. That's a lie. I have been to many a fashion trade party where the premise is that you give away stuff you don't want for tokens to use to get stuff other people have cast off. It is a futile process, as you leave with more stuff you may never wear. As they say: I have no regrets in life, just lessons learnt.

Perhaps at some point in your life you have been shopping, come home with a fabulous dress which, it turned out, you could only wear once because the shape changed after one wash, and you couldn't for love nor money iron out those now permanent creases. If so, this guide is for you. If you have ever bought a T-shirt which twists in shape as you are wearing it, this is definitely for you. Bought a new winter coat which has left you shivering at night like you're getting a fever? Argh! Keep reading. All over the world this is happening, with more and more international fashion retailers in our midst, though it is not only them but also high-end labels using synthetics with poor fabric recovery. If you know what you are buying and its end use, you'll be more successful in obtaining what you need. Whether you spend a small amount on an item for just that one special occasion, or whether you spend a lot on that failsafe dress that lasts, you may want that LBD (little black dress) to work as hard as its fibres can possibly work before it has its very own breakdown in years to come.

A sales assistant in Aldo once said this to me: 'If you find a pair of shoes that do the job and can be worn every day of the season, buy two.' It is a rule people who work in the fashion industry can afford to follow, once they redeem their discount (or a friend's), but one regular folk perhaps can't, whether due to limitations of space or money. Fashion changes every season, although the argument that originality has died is often exemplified on the high street; simple design features from yesteryear almost always return.

Boots come back each season for winter. Mid-calf height, knee, and over the knee are indicative of autumn/winter fashion. However, AW2021/22 platform details were the additional must-have trend. Trying to find a pair of boots without a platform or chunky sole was like trying to get blood from a stone. Impossible. Same with the pale colour scheme of white, cream and stone boots, and with Chelsea detailing, which saw its big revival some years ago. Fashion and function have really come together in the past few years; saying that, the brief revival of cowboy boots in AW2020/21 may not have hit either of these. Not everyone can get away with a cowboy boot, but if you can, line-dance your way through life with confidence.

Lastly, there's the 'one-year rule'. You have all probably been told this before at least once in your life, when it comes to expensive dinnerware sets, crystal glassware, coffee machines, sewing machines, drills, etc. It will be something which you may have blown the dust off once or twice before moving to another surreptitious corner of your spare room, bedroom, kitchen, attic, or cellar. The rule goes: 'if you haven't used it or even attempted to use it in a year, you probably never will'. True? That's my version, others vary. So, do yourself a favour and pass that problem on. I am a firm believer in giving things away to anyone who will benefit more from them; I always start with friends and family. Ask my sister how many brand-new-with-labels pairs of shoes she has received from me without even a tug of war between us to hand them over. I have also gone shopping in her wardrobe for the same (thanks Josephine). If I haven't attempted to touch them in, say, a year, other than the seasonal reorganisation, and they slip lower and lower on my shoe racks (which stood at approximately five feet tall on completion of this book) then they aren't going to get worn. If family and friends demur, pop them in a bag and give them away to whatever charity you support – cancer, poverty, heart disease, homelessness, or mental disorders. Every little helps. I hope I don't get sued for using that famous supermarket quote, but it's so true I thought I'd risk it.

I have found as a style coach that educating the client is as important as dressing them. A stylist is synonymous with a personal trainer: giving you the workout you need for best results. However, going to a class here or there isn't going to break the habits of a lifetime. A style coach is the trainer and the nutritionist, providing the tutelage on the clothes, what suits you, and, I think most importantly, buying these items for style and substance. Understanding what you are buying, in the context of the brand, fabrics, and country of manufacture, will educate you no end. How you spend your money may change, and I assure you so will your perspective. To enrich this guide with a variety of viewpoints, I enlisted men and women, as regular and irregular as you and me, from all backgrounds, ages, and professions, to share their insights and thoughts on the topics expressed in this book. One of my inspirations came from a light-hearted comment made by my friend Chloe. A statement I told her I would steal and use, as often as my shopping budget would allow.

'I don't like my old clothes; I want new ones.' Chloe, 28 (Accountant)

Look @ the Country of Design

More commonly found in high-end fashion, you may see the country of design printed on the label. When it *is* stated, it is often different from the country of manufacture. There are benefits from knowing the country of design, particularly if you favour a style known to be prevalent in certain brands. If you covet the Italian flamboyance of Versace, or Gucci, for example. Or the down-to-earth style of DKNY from the USA, or the British eccentricity of Vivienne Westwood. The price you pay for a certain design house or location is worked into the price of the article. Next, of course, comes the sewing, stitching, and materials, which if outsourced may also require a separate identification on the label.

Look @ the Country of Origin

Here are some legalities. The country of origin (COO) is the country of manufacture, usually where the item has come from. The country of origin must be printed either on a label inside the garment or onto the item itself. It may not seem like anything of importance, but due to the differences in national and international law, without a COO, import and export would be extremely limited and incredibly difficult. Countries all over the world produce, source, and manufacture products with many end uses. The country-of-origin label is not to be confused with the country in which the garment was designed. Brands from all over the world produce fashion in various countries as well as in their own mother country. It is interesting information to have, particularly, for example, if you are aware of the current economic status of the country, the recent politics associated with the country, or even have a simple desire to support local products. Below are a few countries to note (in no particular order).

China

Made in China is stamped, stitched and embossed on stereos, handbags and just about anything in your home. China is still a rapidly growing country, and is the largest supplier to the world of products produced in bulk. In terms of clothing Shanghai is the most important, just so you know, but you won't get this level of detail on a label. Often China is the chosen COO due to its reputation of being the biggest supplier in the world; it is not necessarily indicative of the quality of products, but the knowledge of where your clothes were made is a useful piece of information to have. If you look through your wardrobe, you may find synchrony of COOs within brands, based on their size, fabrics, and category of clothes.

India

The history of manufacture in India isn't quite as prestigious as in China. It has been caught in a race to deliver the quality other countries are known for, and has lagged; however over the past ten to fifteen years there have been improvements with in-house design and technology used in the processes to achieve a reputation of high quality. There have certainly been blunders in India involving some large-scale retail giants – some have since put precautions in place which put the value of the products being produced at the forefront, but also the treatment of the staff employed within the walls of each company, both at home and abroad.

USA

The USA is a major producer of goods for both home and abroad. The sheer size of North America, with every type of weather, provides ideal conditions for this giant country to manufacture across many retail sectors. It is also noted for its home-grown clothing industry, and more popular culture brands like American Apparel manufacture at home to avoid any level of confusion regarding its source. Designers such as Ralph Lauren were born and bred in New York and have a very rich American-brand DNA.

'I do prefer certain brands because of price point and fit. For example, I'm not familiar with many of the German brand names, so I find high-street stores like Zara to be my best friend. I know my size and I know what kind of value I'm getting.' Shoshannah, 28 (Student)

Japan

This small and densely populated country has a very diverse history. As a manufacturing hub, it is no exception. In a word association game, you may see a motorbike and think Kawasaki – unless you are American (Harley Davidson). A camera, you may go with Nikon, unless you are British (as you know the inventor of the camera was British). There is an amazingly unique reason why Japan remains one of the fashion capitals of the world, stemming from its long culture. The economy, in varying terms, remains in the global top three, and also relies on exports – it is a sense of pride for me to have clothes manufactured in Japan, based on their quality as well as the design. Every fashion capital has their own style, and I think I identify the most with Japanese design; something about the fact that comfort is at the forefront (excluding geta footwear – traditional flat, wooden platforms are not my friends, and I have the scars to prove it). Japan since 1960 has had over-proportional growth within its economy, and fashion is most definitely included in that expansion.

'Having travelled to factories in Europe and India, I have seen the extent to which the country your product is manufactured in can affect the quality/price/wear/longevity of a product.' Sarah, 30 (Designer)

Italy

Italian clothing has a link to the boutique nature of shopping; not being directly associated with *en-masse*, large-scale international production perpetuates this. Italy produces coveted sports cars, shoes, food, wine and coffee, and is also home to many fashion designers, such as Dolce & Gabbana, Versace, and Prada. With high-quality craftsmanship and smaller-scale factories, it is an import hub for fashion. Milan, the fashion capital of Italy, hosts some of the biggest names in fashion. From the big houses to the smaller independent retailers, the possibility of buying a pair of handmade shoes is exceptionally common. Italian materials (such as leathers) are regarded as the best in the world, and are often used on products which are manufactured elsewhere to save costs. For a piece of clothing to be sourced and manufactured in Italy indicates – but does not guarantee – eminence and attention to detail, just because many of the most world-famous fashion houses are of Italian heritage. Also, the country has been referred to as the 'shoe capital of the world', which doesn't do much to dispel its reputation for the best fashion has to offer. When I was living in Milan, I could see just how much pride people took in the quality of their products; for them, paying a premium was justified. Additionally, the quality makes it a bargain – if you think about the investment ratio for each year of use: you gain.

'It made me understand that just because something is made in Italy, it's not always high quality, and vice versa – if something is made in India, it's not always a cheap product. There is no way to know which of these factories a garment was made in. However, I check seam construction, fabric composition, and also look at the consistency in the make between the sizes on the rail.' Sarah, 30 (Designer)

Portugal

Parallels have been made with Italy; however, Portugal has become a more popular country of manufacture for large-scale brands and retail in the past ten years. Its heritage is primarily in leather, but it has grown to diversify in textile also. The footwear industry is a proud part of Portuguese history. Production has increased by over 200 per cent in the past ten years; a shocking amount when we remember that we're dealing with millions of pairs, totalling over 115 million pairs produced to date. There was once a time when Portugal was the primary location for manufacturing shoes in quality and bulk at very affordable prices; how things have changed, especially since adopting the Euro, which increased labour costs. There is a long way to go before it can rival Italy, but it is steadily building its reputation and continuing to making waves.

Romania

Made in Romania is a label becoming more and more prevalent on the high streets. Since it joined the EU in 2007, more and more fashion brands have moved production to Romania, especially high-end brands which are associated with quality products. You may find this label in goods produced for the high street like H&M and Zara, or high end for brands such as D&G – the potential of Romania persists as a result of low EU labour costs and large-scale manufacture resources. The fabrics for some high-end clients may be sourced from Italy, as it is in relatively close proximity. Romania's expansion has hit peaks and troughs but shown a steady overall growth. It is as affected as any other country is by the age-old factors of supply and demand, but with labour costs being comparatively low here, it remains a very attractive market for fashion. Romania is not new to manufacturing, but it's definitely broadening its reach, like a European summertime extending into September.

France

With a longstanding history in fashion, France is the world's fourth biggest industrial producer. Boasting international designers such as Chanel, Dior, Balmain and Hermès, France hosts some of the most luxurious fashion houses in the world, in addition to more modern brands, including Agnès B and urban streetwear brand Pigalle. We use many French phrases in fashion; haute couture, meaning high sewing or high fashion, and prêt-à-porter, meaning ready to wear. Even chic is used in every other fashion and lifestyle blog, OOTD (outfit of the day) article, Instagram post, or Tweet. The textile industry in France has conventionally been the reserve of small- and medium-sized companies, which could yield a higher level of quality control compared to larger international factories churning out thousands of units of each article.

'As a buyer I look at the price, but with my knowledge of what is on trend, understanding the fabric and the wearability of the item, I know what I pay for the product is justifiable.' Angela, 50 (Fashion Buying Assistant)

Germany

Living in Berlin, I can see why it is known for its high immigration (after the USA); Germany is a popular destination for people and businesses because of its strong economy. Berlin is often referred to as the start-up capital. Having lived in Germany for over six years, working for the largest online fashion retailer in Europe, I can see that the reputation of German businesses working in a methodical, honest and practical way is well deserved. In recent years, Berlin especially has become a budding fashion capital, though for sure is more recognisable as a technology one. Innovation in machinery and tech alike puts German companies in a reliable place for manufacturing, especially for the clothes we put on our backs. The largest manufacturing companies by revenue are Volkswagen, followed by Daimler AG, responsible for Mercedes-Benz. Germany is in the top five of the biggest textile and clothing exporters in the world. It is clear with the growth of the market share of fashion retailers that this industry is additionally contributing to the economic stability of the country. With the combination of its long history of manufacturing, textiles, and technology, German factories are a centre of advanced machinery, in both sewing machinery and techniques.

UK

The UK is famous today for many brands and technologies, household names and references including the Aston Martin, fish and chips, and a good cup of tea. In the context of this book on clothing it also includes designers such as Henry Holland, Vivienne Westwood, and the late Alexander McQueen; producing goods of high value and quintessential British style.

The UK has come a long way since the mid-eighteenth century, when the rich imported silks and linen and the poor wore wool, which they often spun themselves. In the UK, the industry has been affected by wars, industrial revolutions and politics; textile production peaked in the 1920s but has never returned to its former glory. There is competition with manufacturers in China and India with lower costs to make higher margins, so it's no surprise that many UK companies outsource their manufacturing. There are some who keep a portion of their manufacturing business in the UK, including brands such as

Lipsy and River Island. This is not only good for the UK economy but is also a source of faster lead times to the consumer, from design room to delivery. No one wants to see a top in a magazine and go to the shops only to have the attendant tell them it's sold out. UK manufacturing can cut lead times in half, which means everyone wins; the company, the UK economy and you – your outfit is sorted, and you can Carrie Bradshaw your entrance in style.

'I get inspiration from magazines like *Vogue*.' Angela, 50 (Fashion Buying Assistant)

It is also pertinent to acknowledge the footwear industry in Norwich, which was at one point the hub of textile and footwear production in England. Companies which were established in the eighteenth century were amongst the contributors, though now there are few factories remaining. The acumen of companies which sought and achieved international business have given Norwich notoriety and accomplishments in its history.

The world is an oyster of options. In a consumer's life, and according to their level of patriotism, products hailing from their native country may boost their appeal; after all, why wouldn't you want to support home-grown products, talent, and self-sufficiency? I have always stood by the wisdom that if a product is made in one of the most expensive countries in the world, like the UK for example, the label should be branded with the flag of that nation, helping to validate the cost if it falls above market median. Well, perhaps nothing quite as crass as that (it would be a marketing nightmare, amongst other things) but you get my point. Investing in manufacturing in your country of residence has some merit, especially if you are going to shop anyway. But that's not ignorant advice – to spend on who you know, but also what you know, keeping in mind the brand, its position from many political and commercial standpoints, the labour in its factories, at home and abroad, its stance on institutional racism, sexism and even religious or sexuality bias. The COO is the starting point, triggering thoughts of the costs of transportation of goods from India to a port in Italy, then on to be shipped internationally, which also begs the question of the carbon footprint they leave behind.

When you learn its country of manufacture, you can begin to question whether you really do know the brand. It's from painful experience I ask you to look at that label before you try anything on and fall in love with it, or it will be that much more painful to leave it back on the rack from whence it came. I have shed a tear in a store for that reason, and I don't need to tell you how embarrassing it was, namely because people heard whimpering from behind a curtain in a changing room. There is nothing worse than seeing viscose as a material on the label, but more on that later. I worked in a store back in the day, and sombre sounds from behind that curtain rarely ended well for the shop assistant.

Go through your wardrobe, and review where your favourite pieces have been manufactured – this is Stage 1. Stage 2 is identifying the fabrics that speak to your ethics and compliment your body. Stage 3 is figuring out how you can be more consistent in buying clothes that fit your ethics, your style and your body.

Look @ the Fabrics

Fabric could have been the first chapter, but I thought it best to ease you in with the 'where' before moving onto the 'what'. This chapter on fabrics and how they fit your body is a very practical one, leaning more towards the styling aspect of this shopping guide. Just so you know: every component of an article should be labelled with its fabric, to complete the total composition on the label. The value of a product is often determined by the fabrics it is comprised of, directly correlated to the item's durability; the workmanship that has gone into the manufacturing process is also just as important. A hand-sewn dress could never rival the fast-fashion industry price-point, and it would never have to.

A textile is synthesised by its fibres, usually within three stages: spinning, weaving, and finishing. There are two types of textile fibre: natural and synthetic. When a garment is mass-produced, there are quality controls which ensure the vast majority of items go out to the public in keeping with a standard the brand represents. So, if a brand sells a silk dress or produces handmade leather footwear, it would be assumed the brand ensures a quality measure in line with the quality of the fabric. Silk is one of the more delicate fabrics. Just as a pair of shoes handmade out of some polyurethane, non-biodegradable sheet of plastic is useless, a badly sewn silk dress is a disaster. It is always sad to see a wool coat with wonky stitching, two T-shirts size M, but both with different widths, or a pair of suedette shoes in a store where one has been bleached by the store lighting. Poor-quality fabric negates its worth and value, as does bad assembly. Just like diamonds, there are varying qualities, but fabrics aren't given a quality rating in the same way, and it is not always so easy to tell on sight alone.

'I love fashion, brands, people, everything that tells a story, moves, doesn't stand still and always strives for innovation; the particular "something", the exact "savoir-faire". For this reason, I seldom go for mainstream, I love high fashion and hereby mix and match. I like to feel, touch and see, I prefer physical stores over online shopping. I have fave brands which I am observing and mainly buy these during sales season. I shop throughout the year for sneakers, tops, and jeans. I have high demands for aesthetics and get influenced by campaigns, which cross-innovate and combine art with fashion and authentic testimonials. E.g., the new CK campaigns make me fly.' Anna (Strategic Marketing & Performance Manager)

Polyester

Polyester was a genius invention to elasticate the clothing industry, and is often used in swimwear, underwear, and trims. It is durable and quick drying. It is an extensively utilised synthetic fabric, often the umbrella term for a polymer of plastic. Polyester comes from a combination of two words in chemistry, polymer (to have many parts) and ester (a chemical compound). Don't worry, that's the biggest portion of pure science I'll be dropping. As you know, plastic does not degrade (or will take an incredibly long time to do so). It has dense fibres with no ventilation for your skin to interact with the atmosphere; this can be a benefit in colder climates, as it is insulating. But remember the best way to keep warm is to wear layers and create pockets of heat – I have poor circulation, and this advice that was given to me from a very young age has stuck with me for decades.

Polyester is often more affordable than natural fibres for items such as coats and soft accessories, also often mixed with natural fibres for durability and reducing production costs, though these reductions are not always fed back through to the consumer in the retail price. If you want a cashmere coat – or, should we say, a coat advertised as cashmere – the best idea is to always check the composition and ascertain whether it is combined with a polyester. Ten per cent cashmere does not a cashmere coat make. Imagine you were told just 10% of a joke, paid 10% of your salary or watched 10% of your favourite movie – these would all be deal-breakers! Rebecca Bloomwood famously bought a coat with a recessive cashmere gene (in the film adaptation of the book *Confessions of a Shopaholic*) and the pain was felt through the screen. Whether at full retail value or on discount – check what you are paying for. Polyester is a big resource for the clothing industry because it retains its colour and shape, and will be here even after the cockroaches go belly up.

Polyester and synthetics are produced from petroleum-based chemicals otherwise known as petrochemicals. Joining the small molecules to produce polymers is via a chemical reaction. This goes beyond the Bunsen burner tricks you would do at secondary school; the scale this process works on uses chemicals that you should not work on in the lab. The process of synthetic material manufacture is regarded as a major contributor to greenhouse gas emissions (CO_2), with the incredible energy required to join the polymer also considered to have a large impact on the effects of global warming. One benefit to its production is that polyester can be synthesised anywhere in the world, and can reduce the costs of shipping fabrics. Another benefit, which is offset by the disadvantages of its ingredients and manufacturing process, is that synthetic fabrics do not require plants as a resource. So, if possible, recycled polyester is an option, to endorse a more sustainable future for this fabric.

'If it is a mainstream brand like H&M, I check the care label to avoid artificial fibres like polyester, acrylic...' Anna (Strategic Marketing & Performance Manager)

Nylon and Acrylics

Another synthetic polymeric fabric is nylon (remember it from chemistry at school?), a fabric produced from oil and coal; this non-biodegradable component is used in abundance in the textile industry. No fancy reason for its naming, with *nyl* given as an arbitrary assignment, and the ending -*on* added to keep it akin with other fabric names e.g., cotton and rayon. There are no holes in the fabric, and therefore it is impermeable. Post patent in 1937, it was hailed as an indestructible fibre, because it will last forever. Goodness, clothes from the past eighty-five years hanging around. Forever. It is not, however, indestructible, as you know if you have experienced the fury yourself of a pair of nylon hosiery getting a ladder at the most inappropriate time and place.

Regarding acrylics, I am still wearing a blouse of my mother's from somewhere in the seventies, and it looks as new as the day she was pictured in it. Fifty years on and my vintage is still going. The word isn't just assigned to fabrics as you know, it is used too for paint, nails and toys to name a few other products – utilised for fabrics, fibres, plastics and paint. The original meaning of the word acrylic comes from Latin, but its use today as a completely synthetic material is due to the fact it is synthesised from acrylic acid. It is often hailed as an alternative fabric for clothing and accessories due to allergies or aversions from wool or natural fibres, but its durability better be worth it with its longevity, otherwise that gifted ugly winter woolly hat will have to make its guest appearance every year for the rest of your life.

'I tend not to buy goods that are dry-clean only, due to my easy lifestyle. But I typically only buy cottons and wools in jumpers. I once bought a Pull and Bear 100% acrylic jumper and I regret everything about it.' Michael, 28 (Fashion Merchandiser)

Cotton

Cotton is a natural textile, grown from the ground and thought to be the oldest fibre ever used. The fabric allows air to circulate and so your skin can breathe, which is just one of the benefits; it is also very durable and skin comfortable. Additionally, it is absorbent, providing a natural way to let damp and heat escape rather than trapping moisture in. Don't worry, I'm not going to tell you how you can grow, spin and stitch your very own pair of jeans (yes, denim is cotton – some people are still in the dark about that one). I will, however, give you all the rant I have given my extended family, friends, colleagues, and clients from the very early stages of when I was working on a retail shop floor. No matter how you treat, condition, or dye a piece of cotton – whether it be for a pair of jeans, a designer T-shirt or a plain grey jumper with a brand's logo on it – they all originate from a plant, not from unicorn tears. Depending on whether extensive treatments have been applied, just the fact that there is a certain branded decal sewn onto the chest, a rear or belt loop, should not automatically earn it a retail price in triple digits. You may be paying a markup for the brand, in addition to the production costs of the item. Whether fabrics are being shipped to different locations is also a contributing factor for high-priced cotton products. Remember that super-short chapter at the beginning? Having an article designed in one country, then produced in another with fabrics shipped there can be an expensive set of logistics. It is difficult per item to be aware of these finite details, but what is certain is that cotton production is dominated by the USA, followed by China and India. Cotton naturally grows in warmer climates.

Cotton has had a chequered history, starting with the free labour that picked cotton for hundreds of years in the USA under slavery, a well-known historical detail. Cotton has also come under fire in the recent past for its negative impact on the environment. Through modern technology, high annual yields can be accomplished via the use of synthetic fertilisers or pesticides. This can inject harmful chemicals not only into the soil but also into the air and water – we humans are 70% water and have that reflex of breathing, which makes it a big problem for us all. As well as this, there is the copious amount of water used to produce high yields of cotton. This is a very brief summary, with nowhere near all the details of the negative impacts of cotton production on the environment.

As I have always said, if you don't build it, they won't come – you have the option of cutting out the textile completely, but this isn't necessary. I am sure you have a few items hanging in your wardrobe as we speak – these days even the big brands have opted for organic cotton within their ranges, but do your research: does their code of ethics prevent the use of harmful chemicals in their fashion production, for example? The perfect balance is being able to enjoy the style and aesthetics of a brand whose ethics you also agree with. Perhaps you are already that lucky. Otherwise, start at where you have bought cotton from in the past and check out their stance on cotton production. They will probably have an organic or recycled option, or a blend of the two, but just note it will be a bit pricier than the average cost of your regular crew-neck white tee.

Linen

Linen, a fabric often worn by detectives on US TV in the 1980s, with colourful crew-neck T-shirts and big hair. As well as any man who ever got married in a Hollywood romcom movie on the beach, usually in Hawaii. Linen is a textile produced from the flax plant, and is ideal for warmer climates due to its light nature and its breathability. A pain in the ass to iron, but I guess that is the nature of the beast. Sometimes it is combined with polyester to reduce the amount of creasing. Linen suits go in and out of what is considered 'fashionable', but they are always more functional. Due to its high maintenance, it is more of a luxury fabric, but in essence it has a purpose and is ideal for it. It's often more expensive than regular cotton, even the organic variety – but you should always look for 100% linen as its function may be impaired when combined with other textiles. The manufacturing process is much more time-intensive than for cotton. China is the biggest producer of linen worldwide, though throughout Europe, too, countries are producing high-quality linen. Linen is strong and lasts long, even more so than cotton as a result of the cellulose fibres. It isn't as soft as cotton, but damn it you can't help but feel like a grown-up in linen. Adults also think about longevity more, and linen is a textile for that.

As a top up of information on one of my absolute favourite fabrics, there are also different types, which make them more appropriate for different functions. This isn't a need to know, but more so things you may want to know:

- Damask linen: although the most delicate variety, it still embodies the signature linen strength but with the beauty of a more delicate fabric, making it perfect for ornate furnishings like tablecloths

- Plain-woven: a sturdy option most utilised for dish towels and reusable napkins

- Closely woven: the USP for this is type of linen is its softness, making it an ideal candidate for clothing and bedding

- Loose weave: this type is the most absorbent, so also used for napkins but it is less durable, so maybe only once-a-year-at-Christmas napkins, as opposed to every Sunday roast.

Silk

Made from the product of silkworms, and more often than not associated with decadence. Silk was often worn by the rich in old sixteenth-century England – think shiny thighs and big shoulders. It is a fabric which has a clinging and static quality, so caution is advised. The main difficulty is with cleaning it; many washing machines have a setting for silk, and even one for wool (below). However, the integrity of the garment after machine washing will be determined by the integrity of the brand, and on the washing machine, to be honest. If it states you can use the silk setting by all means do, just don't forget how delicate the item is. The price point for silk can vary widely; you can find a 100% silk blouse in a high-street store under £90 (€100 /$100), and in a high-end boutique for five times the amount.

Choosing a silk is like choosing a girlfriend in the nineties – which one has the best weave? Jokes aside, traditionally the best silk garments come from fabric which has been produced with one iridescent, shiny side, and the opposite dull for strength and quality. Then you should also consider the fact that silk is a tough fabric to work with, and that sewing it will prove tricky (same way, I imagine, you can identify a snitch in prison, the one with the best stitches. OK, jokes over). Mulberry silkworm silk is possibly the most well-known type, and often the silk of choice – if it's written on the label, great. If not… well, now we start getting into the nitty gritty of what to ask the sales assistant, customer service, or feedback service. If you want to get technical, the cost versus the quality of silk can be ascertained by the price, but also whether you are getting value for your money, for which you can ask for the momme weight. A high momme weight means a thicker fabric and a greater density, but not always a higher quality of silk. When referring to clothing up top – shirts, blouses, etc. – 15–22 momme is respectably standard. A chiffon blouse typically, however, goes up to 8 momme, crêpe de Chine up to 16, and charmeuse up to 30. When dealing with bedding and upholstery the question is which momme is fit for purpose, depending on the end use. For bedding, a fabric no less than 22 should last the test of time for those good night sleeps, as well as the, let's say, more exciting ones.

'I can't seem to warrant spending the money on something that might be so unique I only wear once. I have been burned a few times so now just go with what I'm comfortable in and stop trying to kid myself that I'll get loads of use out of a really crazy printed jumper, for example. The investment pieces I do have in my wardrobe tend to be leather shoes from brands like Folk or

Whistles. I get them resoled when they need so they last longer.'
Sarah, 30 (Designer)

Wool

Wool is a natural textile fibre taken from sheep, who even on the high hills of windy Wales never seem to catch a chill. Why is this, you ask? The insulating properties of the fabric create pockets of heat, whilst allowing your skin to breathe. Other animals can also be used to produce mohair and cashmere (goats) as well as angora (rabbits). Wool is knitted into various types of knit to create a multitude of clothing; jumpers, coats, cardigans, even trousers. It is also a composite in hats – lest we forget, most body heat is lost through your head, so this may be a fortunate requirement for a woolly beanie hat or trilby. Australia, China, the USA and New Zealand are all big producers of wool globally.

The sentiment attached to wool over synthetics is that it is traditionally worn for warmth, it is permeable and insulating and has been used as a fabric for thousands of years. It is this, in addition to the farming of the animals, which means manufacturers can demand a higher price point than alternative plastics. It is desirable, but for sure not the least expensive for maintenance; the purchase of mothballs alone may be a single cause to pass it over. OK, there have been more modern inventions since mothballs, but they are all deterrents to the beautiful creatures. I remember like it was yesterday. It was the winter of 2015. Excited by the chill in the air and the requirement for a heavier layer to wrap around my neck, I pulled down the box, which was clearly perforated with a hole the size of a flying wool assassin. When I pulled out my favourite Burberry wool scarf with a hole the size of a one pence piece, my heart broke a little.

Enough about me, back to wool. It doesn't wrinkle per se, given a good stretch. It's also a pretty resistant fabric, durable to no end, and even fire resistant. Keeps you warm in cold temperatures, and as a result of its properties impeding heat transfer, keeps you cool too. I always fall back to thinking of those resilient creatures, sheep and others, found in sometimes the harshest weather conditions on the globe. Wool is classified as an eco-textile, being renewable and sustainable. Can we say *slow down* to that climate change please?

So, if you see wool, and it's not normally your go-to – give it a try. 'But it is so itchy,' I heard someone say once. This is not a rule of thumb, and is a result of how it is treated as a raw material. If you want to sound like a proper smarty pants in a store, I dare you ask what the measurement of microns is – a higher number is associated with the itchy feeling, based on the diameter of the strands of wool. Everyone's skin is different, with varying levels of sensitivity, so this one is more of a hands-on test – but if you have the measurement of microns available go with the lowest for what is likely to be a softer-feeling wool. As a reference to start from, ultra-fine merino fleece can have fibres as tight as 10 microns in diameter – increasing in diameter you get superfine, fine, medium, and strong merino, which can go above 23 microns.

'I tend not to wear wool unless it's cashmere or merino as I have sensitive skin. Also, I'm not a fan of scuba fabrics. If I had Kim K's body, I would wear latex.' Shoshannah, 28 (Student)

Viscose

My least favourite textile of all time, in all multiverses, is viscose. Its primary source is natural (cellulose from pine trees) then via several processes it is whipped into viscose, the wispy fly-away fabric we have come to know and, regretfully, buy today. My distaste for it is largely because it is prone to becoming misshapen during its initial wear or after one wash, and it just doesn't provoke confidence in a second outing. Call it bad luck or a rigorous washing regime, but it is the supervillain in my comic book universe. If you find viscose in the label of anything you want to buy, and you love the print, design and cut that much you still really want that item, by all means buy it, but you might want to buy two or three replacements at the same time. I'm just saying, you have been warned. My best advice is to go to your own closet and have a look at the labels which have viscose as the primary fabric, and see if it has done you proud thus far. If so, by Jove it is a miracle, by way of a heavily treated textile. If not, it may be something to consider next time you are in the shops.

My distaste for viscose stems from the fact that not only does it lose its strength when wet (back to becoming misshapen after a wash); it is flammable and has poor crease recovery. It is like an enchantress, taking on different guises, posing as cotton, silk, velvet, and taffeta. Soaking up dyes to lure you in, like the witch in Hansel and Gretel, with vibrant colours and prints, all lit up like a house made of sweets. Once you're sucked in to buying it, though, the piece of clothing might, like the witch, find itself disposed of in the most heinous of ways – maybe not burnt alive in an oven, but there's always the clothes-for-cash bin at 50p a kilogram. Its popularity, being in the top five most commonly used textiles in the world, means this is a PSA! If the properties of viscose weren't reprehensible enough, it is also a driver in the fast fashion industry – farms for viscose production are not only treated with harmful chemicals to increase yield but are also responsible for the destruction of woodland. When I was young (along with inventions like the wheel) it used to be industry that would create demand with the right supply, but that ship has well and truly sailed. Now, the demand for this daily changing world of social media is causing supply to be the driver, and it is spilling over the proverbial edge and bleeding all over us all. As I said, totally your choice – but if you are looking for direct affordable alternatives, I would suggest that any alternative fabric would be an improvement, even polyester.

Real fur

Companies can recycle – or upcycle, as the newer term may be – real animal fur to create new garments and accessories, whereby the fur is being reclaimed or reused. (I think nowadays the term 'recycled' is used to imply products outside of the clothing industry.)

There are charities and organisations who would say not to wear fur under any circumstances. Although it is our choice if we want to buy real fur today, an informed assessment of how the animal fur was obtained should always accompany a purchase, as without it there is the possibility that more sectors than just the clothing industry are being funded by the acquisition. This is in addition to the inhumane operations which go on in fur farms where animals endure cruel and painful practices. Without finger pointing, being informed is never a bad thing. With vintage furs, it is a lot more difficult to ascertain its provenance and so, in my humble opinion, it is reasonable to say that what was done more than fifty years ago is done. Global warming takes no prisoners, and my first winter in Germany demanded fewer man-made materials and more of a natural approach. You may hold the opposing opinion, not condoning it but we are too far away from an 88 mph DeLorean time machine to do anything to change what has already happened.

Fur's appeal, apart from aesthetics, is its durability and its extraordinary warmth. Real fur coats, vests and accessories are sourced from rabbit, fox, mink, muskrat, chinchilla, and possum, among other animals. There are also reports of cat, dog and even beaver fur. The process by which the furry animal pelt is turned into a beautiful item isn't great reading material, so I won't go there. But what I would say is animal cruelty should never be excused, for fashion, food or otherwise. Whilst I wear real vintage fur, these are items that I have inherited and seldom bought myself. If ever I was to make a purchase any point forward (which I doubt), I endeavour to do my due diligence to ensure it was sourced as a bi-product first, and secondly the food farm was also not practicing cruel practices to increase yield or profit on their products.

Real fur can be sold on a popular fashion market stall or in a designer boutique – either way the price can still vary extensively, whether new, vintage or upcycled. If you will cross that bridge, look out for the lining fabric: is it thin and likely to rip against the weight of the article? Look at the stitching: is it straight and tight with no fraying edges? And for the love of Homer J Simpson, *ask* when buying, or do your research and see whether the brand is caught up in any unethical farming of animals.

Synthetic Fur

If your moral compass just says no to the real thing, the beautiful fur look can still be accomplished with synthetics, which can be dyed and styled to a multitude of cuts, shapes and prints. Synthetic, faux or fake fur has multiple uses for its aesthetic and feel (especially in furniture). It won't keep you as warm as real fur, but it has the illusion of opulence. Since its commercial peak in the 1950s, you can now get faux fur in a variety of colours, prints and lengths, in coats, accessories and even as an adornment on footwear. As above, pay special attention to the lining and stitching. Faux fur is also referred to as a pile fabric, made from polymeric fibres which undergo a complex process to mimic the specific type of fur required. Much like other synthetic fabrics, the capacity for your body to breathe is inhibited. From the faux-fur coat to the faux-fur rug, it can be enjoyed by all – from the catwalks to the DIY home store, faux fur is animal-friendly so rest assured, you should never have an activist throw a can of blood-red paint over you, *Sex and the City*-style! So, enjoy!

'If I'm looking for something in particular i.e., a new cardigan, I look at sites like Lyst.com, on which I can be really specific about the item I'm after and they show me all the choices from numerous brands.' Sarah, 30 (Designer)

Leather

The hide of an animal is processed into what we know as leather. From the time of our ancestors (Neanderthals, if you believe in Darwinism), it was used because of its properties of retaining heat, as well as being robust and flexible. It is used across the fashion industry; any item of clothing can be made from real leather and probably has, all the way to the leather tee. With such desirable qualities, it is also used in stationery and upholstery for homes and offices. There are several tanning processes which turn the hides into the leather we use daily – but this is not printed on labels within the clothes. Some processes are rarer and more complicated, which may escalate the price of an item compared to its apparently similar counterpart. Knowledge of the tanning process may be known by a sales advisor, supervisor or manager for a high-end retailer or designer store but do not expect to get this information from your local high-street store you will be barking up the wrong tree. I advise you ask which type of leather it is – as in, which animal, if it is not stated in the label – but you may be able to tell by physical appearance or touch.

Cattle is the most common source of leather; however, cheaper leathers from pig and goat are also used. The quality of the animal is a major determinant of the end-quality of leather, defined in many cases by the conditions on the farm and the nourishment the animal receives. Leather from cattle can be a by-product of the meat industry, but there are also manufacturers using cattle primarily for leather. Popularity for leather may have had its peak in the eighties, with the Michael Jackson red leather 'Thriller' outfit – the icon, the legend, the red leather suit. Moving through the nineties, in Dr Marten-style lace-up military boots, to any number of articles including the black leather biker jacket, which is a staple item for the next millennium.

Pig leather can be identified by the pin dot pox on its surface; for footwear it is often used inside the shoe, as leather lining, to decrease the cost whilst maintaining the 100% leather branding of the shoe. Pig is also used in bags and belts, but seldom in clothing like coats and jackets – best to tap out of a full pig-leather jacket which could otherwise be made in higher quality leathers.

Deer is super soft and malleable, ideal for both clothing and accessories, in tees and gloves. Great for a snug, body-hugging fit. If you have the feeling you are putting down Bambi's mum, you can forgo this option.

Buffalo is a large animal, its leather commonly associated with being thick and incredibly durable; hence its widespread use in furniture. My mum picked out possibly the sexiest, most durable sofa set some years ago, a tan buffalo-leather three-piece suite to house the bums of her seven kids, guests, and seven hyperactive grandchildren. An investment for the future, if I ever saw one. It is a hardwearing leather, great for baggage and footwear that needs that tough-as-nails appeal.

Believe it or not, that delicious pink fish the salmon is the most commonly used amongst fish leathers; mostly for aesthetics. Often made as a by-product of the salmon food industry, and thus sustainable in this respect, it can be stronger than cow leather, with its sexy one-direction cross-fibre structure. Be prepared to pay for these executive advantages.

Crocodile skin is used in clothes and accessories almost like a trophy head on a wall. These animals were hunted by the old beloved movie character Crocodile Dundee – those below thirty years old at this stage may need Google at their disposal, but here is a picture – remember now? Check out those classy teeth around his hat.

As a young, impressionable, teenage fashionista, ostrich was my favourite leather. Often used in handbags in magazines and TV shows, it was always worn by A-list celebrities, and designed by the haute-couture fashion houses. The look was always so exclusive and rare, and as a student at university studying Medical Biology, it was definitely out of my reach.

Back to the ostrich. This type of leather is often farmed from African ostriches, primarily South African. Now as much as I would hope all farming for feathers, skin, and meat is performed under free-range conditions, we all know this isn't the case. This beautiful leather has bumps or empty quill follicles, my first encounter with the reality of the production of such products for the fashion industry. A high-cost value leads directly to a high retail value – which in turn creates its own exclusivity and luxury. Often selectively bred for desirable characteristics, there are now under a million bred ostriches left in the world – its exclusivity is not just a concept, it is a fact!

As vegans do not consume or wear animal products, I want to openly state that these chapters aren't meant to be provocative but informative, to help better understand the uses of leather, wool and fur, from environmental and animal cruelty standpoints. Other meat-eating folk may also be aware of the improper conditions for animals on farms, which have reduced consumers' confidence in these products for the clothing industry. There are negative impacts of animal products on global warming and excessive farming damaging the environment – this is no lecture, just information. We are in an age in which plastic bags are taxed across Europe, and change is happening slowly. If we all do our part and slow down the pace of fashion, our informed choices can make a big impact.

With all of that said, I am of the opinion that animal products should still be used for the fashion industry. Animal textiles can be sustainable, recyclable and biodegradable, as opposed to some of their synthetic counterparts. Some textiles, leathers for example, can be produced as a by-product of the meat industry and are very durable. The benefits are there. The problem arises when their production, high demand and disposal can turn a craft dating back as far as 3000 BC to a more unethical method of creating high yields. I've had the same leather DKNY bag for fifteen years (a classic envelope chain bag) and have never needed to update it; I hope to be wearing it for another fifteen. We have the choice, not only of which products to buy, but also the speed at which to keep purchasing.

Mixed Fabrics

It is commonplace for fabrics to be made out of a combination of fibres, to maximise the benefits and minimise the disadvantages. A stronger, more durable fabric which takes well to dyes and is iron-friendly? You're in a world of make-believe if you think it could exist without having a dark side. Cotton and linen are often mixed together, as is polyester, with natural fibres in general. Mixed textiles don't necessarily downgrade the quality, and are often used to increase durability or reduce shrinkage. Regardless of this, mixing synthetics with natural fabric reduces their renewability, and may ultimately add to the ever-increasing polymer mountains in landfill dumps.

Not to go too deep, but there has been a negative opinion about mixing fabrics for some time. The Bible recommends against it – specifically stating 'do not put on a garment woven with two different kinds of threads' (Lev. 19:19). Now, there are other recommendations from the Bible which modern-day law sees some common sense in –

there is the murder thing, which is big, illegal everywhere, as is theft. Still stigmatised but enforced less by law is adultery, for example. But this fabric one seems a bit leftfield. It refers specifically to the mixture of wool and linen, and there are many theories as to why this rule was passed. Some suggest that it was only permitted for royalty and not the commoner; others have no idea, as linen and wool aren't a commonplace mixed textile. As interesting as you may or may not have found this, I guess that last bit of trivia is something to mention at a party, starting with 'Did you know…?'

Look @ the Washing Label

It is annoying to find that perfect item you come to wear and love, and have succeeded in impressing Dave in Accounts with, but now it needs a wash before it's ready to be envied another day. Instead of blindly bunging it in the machine with its like-coloured products you check the washing care label… fecking heck it's dry-clean only. Giant meh. It's time-consuming, and possibly not worth the investment after you end up paying its retail value in dry-cleaning bills for a few months. The main reason a fabric will not be suitable for the washing machine these days is that it is fragile, like viscose. The machine may even be too harsh on the gentle setting, and will ruin the integrity of the garment, either after one wash or over time.

'I mostly follow washing instructions when cleaning my clothes. I am guilty of using the gentle cycle when a care label says "Dry clean only".' Shoshannah, 28 (Student)

Here is a pretty comprehensive guide you can paste above the washing machine, or download with the electronic copy of this book to have on your shopping trips in the good old-fashioned stores.

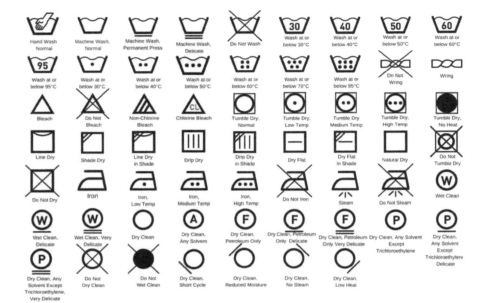

'I've made a lot of expensive mistakes in the past, so experience helps the way I shop and buy. Re: bags, there is always a selling benefit for an additional removable strap from a bucket bag or shopper to an across-body. The customer just needs to be informed of it. If I buy shoes, I prefer boxed as that's the way I store them.' Angela, 50 (Fashion Buying Assistant)

Machine Wash

This remains the most conventional way of cleaning your clothes. Depending on how sophisticated it is, whether it has a WiFi connection, Bluetooth, or whether it simply reads your mind, you should have the basic temperature settings as above. It can be a quick wash of thirty minutes to an hour, a longer wash to get out heavy stains which shall not be spoken of here, and other settings to accommodate different fabrics. It is basically our modern version of the quintessential, once held dear household appliance, the washboard. For those who have to Google this appliance, it was a ridged board, on which you would gain the best guns by pounding your clothes into water and scrubbing the dirt away with brute force.

Hand Wash

There is the traditional hand wash you can still perform with your mitts, not using a washboard – seen here – of course, it would negate the handwash setting. Call it old fashioned, but there are still some articles of clothing which require a bit of TLC. This setting generally requires cool water and a mild detergent. Whether using a basin or the bathroom sink, a five-minute hand wash can really extend the longevity of some pieces. I became a hand-wash convert when my bra hook tore a wide hole in my favourite top of the season when rolling round in the machine. It wasn't the fault of my bra, and I couldn't begrudge it – a hook was made to hook. But since then, I separately hand wash my bras (unless they go in the machine with my gym clothes, which I couldn't care less about – if they come out with a hole, sure I will be less aerodynamic but it will create a breeze hole for better cooling whilst working out. There's always a silver lining). Alternatively, a mesh laundry bag can be used in the gen-pop wash cycle, just don't overstuff them. They are often made out of plastic; if you prefer a natural textile, use a pillowcase closed with safety pins for your delicate bits.

Dry Cleaning

This is a cleaning method used by professionals, where you can launder your clothes and textiles using solvents instead of good old faithful water. It is not actually a dry process; fabrics are soaked in a substance, the most commonly used being tetrachloroethylene. As mentioned above in the specific fabric chapters, some textiles cannot stand the trauma of being washed in water, like viscose – it simply gives up and has a breakdown, figuratively speaking. Natural fibres like wool can change their shape in a standard wash. Dry cleaning is also an alternative to using elbow grease and cleaning with your hands. It is always written explicitly in the label if the item is delicate, but if your washing machine doesn't have the delicate, wool, or cool wash function and a hand wash isn't part of your weekly routine, dry cleaning may become a reality and an addition to your weekly expenses instead. Food for thought when falling in love at first sight with an item in the shop.

Detergents

In any supermarket there is a wide range of detergents. Depending on your budget and skin sensitivity, going with the most organic brand protects not only your skin but also the water supply. I have been a non-bio detergent shopper for years, mainly due to the fact that whatever enzymes added to detergents to help break down the proteins, fat and whatnot found in food stains and who knows what else, simply did not agree with me and my upper dermis. There is also the fact that there may be some damage to the natural fibres being eaten away at – not just all those chocolate stains from the brownie you treat yourself to from the amazing bakery down the road… There are also sensitive detergents for sensitive skin (often with a picture of a chunky baby on the front) – these are child-friendly, although this is often not explicitly written. With the removal of perfume and dyes you may have naturally derived ingredients used, making it an alternative detergent which is gentle on your skin.

It is a fact that at some point you will discover the power of bleach and how it strips the colour from a dyed fabric. Applying this logic, many use it to regain an item's white brilliance. However, bleach is not only a strong, toxic chemical to then wrap around your flesh, one that can potentially cause irritation as a mild side effect, but it also has a pungent smell, it is corrosive and has been known to be a cause of household poisoning. When combined with other cleaning products it is possible for it to release dangerous gases, and if used carelessly it can do damage to your load of colours – think of the blacks turning brown, the fading of your reds and the vibrant yellows dulling like a cloud over the sun.

Look @ the Drying Instructions

Whether a fabric should be put in the dryer or not should appear on the care label with instructions. However, the impact this will have if you choose to ignore the label is dependant not only on the quality of the fabric, but its age and composition. Some of you are blessed with gardens, in which to dry your laundry in the nature of the world, getting that neighbourhood breeze through your pants. Others are blessed with a dryer, and get to enjoy the perils of ironing as an additional job to the turmoil of daily life as a human adult. Others go to the launderette and also enjoy the perils of creased laundry. There's flat drying in the house – on the balcony, hanging from the shower curtains, over a chair, on the radiator. Did I miss something? Hanging from the door? Well, whatever method you use, have a peek at the recommendations before you demand your partner lose 2 kg so he can fit into his shrunken wool jumper (sorry hubby – I got distracted).

The Dryer

There are several benefits of using the dryer. Lint removal, the fact that it's quick, and if required it can cancel out the sound of people you live with, etc. It should not, however, be used on certain fabrics, including high-elastane products, as it can destroy the resilience of the item. Look for the fabric composition of the product – any more than 10% elastane, and I wouldn't use the dryer, especially if the item is of any value. It also adds heat, so wool and some cottons may see some shrinkage after one too many dryer excursions.

'I do look at the care label because I've had a few experiences of shrunken rompers and sweaters. Also, I want my clothes to last as long as possible and I think proper care is key.' Shoshannah, 28 (Student)

Air / Aerial / Flat dry

This is a method of drying wool, animal fabrics, household items like bathmats (with a rubber back) and other fabrics which may change shape after washing. If it isn't stated on the care label, assume that you can bung the item in the dryer or put it out to hang dry with the rest of the weekly laundry. Air drying takes the longest, especially inside a home with no natural air flow – like in my first Berlin home: a fourth-floor apartment with no balcony, in a minus-ten-degree winter. I'm not bitter, just stating facts. The central heating will give it a kick nonetheless.

Radiator / Heater

This often gives that crispy, rough texture that feels like gravel, something particularly undesirable in towels, flannels, anything that touches you – ain't nobody got time for that! These crispy results are intensified when the item has been washed in hard water; the minerals in hard water also do no favours for maintaining the brilliance of white clothes.

Look @ the Fasteners, Buttons and Joiners

First, look to make sure you have a spare somewhere on the inside of the garment. Not a zip, that would be oh-too generous, but for buttons and other fasteners, you should find a spare, often hanging with the care label. I'm not advising you to take a spare-button thief shopping with you, but during the production and pre-purchase lifecycle of an article, being tried on and moved around, not all will survive with that spare intact.

Zips

The best manufacturer of zips in the world is YKK, a fastener company established over 75 years ago. If you buy any coat, pair of boots, handbag, anything from a designer brand or high-end label, or anything for which you want assurance it will last the test of time, there is one manufacturer's stamp you can rely on and be assured of its quality. Department stores such as Harrods have refused to stock companies who do not use YKK zips – fact. Branding is key with many retailers; having a branded GAP zip or a Zara button would be the preferred choice over YKK. In their own words, YKK use the best materials, made by the most modern equipment and mass-produced under extreme quality control. They rate their attaching machines as 'dependable'. The company also provides experienced advice on attaching methods, reinforcement and seam location to ensure that fasteners are attached properly to your garments.

Buttons

Buttons, as used as a fastener, are not to be confused with the USA term 'button', which are what Brits refer to as 'badges'. Now, a little history on the button, ancient examples of which have been found as far back as 2800 BC. Ancient Romans used materials like wood and bronze to fasten their hefty garments back in the day. Today, plastic is the common material for these trusty closures. Buttons are generally easier and cheaper to fix than zips, something to think about for the longevity of any purchase. The ordeal of having to repair a zip on a pair of knee-high boots is one everyone would rather not have to go through. Same goes for your handbag, or your favourite winter coat in the middle of January – or any time, to be honest. Buttons were here before the zip, and by George they will be here after. The worst thing is a button falling off on the first wear, so examine buttons before purchasing and for goodness' sake look for that free extra one which any self-respecting brand will have inside the garment. Two, if you are lucky.

Snap Fastener / Poppers

Poppers (aka pearl snaps or press studs) are a wonderful invention for speed and ease. Modern snap fasteners were first patented by German inventor Heribert Bauer in 1885 as the 'Federknopf-Verschluss', a novelty fastener for men's trousers. Its unique connection is comprised of a circular lip under a disc which fits into a groove on the top of another, holding the two fast until a certain amount of force is applied. This fastener's pair of interlocking discs are usually made from metal, but plastic is an alternative. Be careful: there should be a clause, when garments come with snap fastenings, that with thinner fabrics they should be reinforced otherwise they are prone to rip. Any sewing enthusiast should know snaps are not ideal for loose knits, so when it's sale time after Christmas and you see that long rail of the same knit just check what fastener they all have.

Magnetic Fasteners

The magnetic closure is more common on handbags and purses, as a quick fastener for the open tote, clutch, shopper, and wallet. Magnetic fasteners close with limited fuss and hassle, due to the convenience of the magnetic attraction of the two sides with each other. Depending on the strength of the magnets and how accurately they are aligned on both sides, though, they can prove ineffective as a closure at all. Ever had that fiddle, with elbows at three and nine, trying to close that magnetic button, looking like you are going crazy with a bit of fabric? If done right, they can be the easiest solution, faster and more convenient than a zip or popper, which often requires two hands to complete the regular task of closing one's bag or jacket.

Look @ the Clothes

Clothing is so broad a category, covering everything that forms the next layer of fabric over your underwear (and including the underwear itself!). Due to laws put in place by governing bodies around the world, clothing is an absolute necessity in the majority of public places, but can also be one of the greatest luxurious immoderations in the world. In magazines, on billboards, buses, and especially in stores, there are pictorial messages of the latest fashions, showing you what is in fashion, which type of skirt, cut-off top, or jeans modelled on someone aspirational to inform the consumer on what to wear and how to wear it to stay in style. Fashion jargon is thrown at us as if part of the syllabus, after geography and before maths. Understanding these terms, definitions and even fashion idioms come with your level of devotion to the industry, so people tell me by their blissful ignorance. The more you know the less necessary clothes may appear, and seem more and more an indulgence.

We obviously want to know what the fancy terms are and how the clothes fit. At the very least, having the confidence to simply communicate with a sales assistant and actually know what the hell they are talking about as they try to convince you of what's in and what trends best accommodate your figure is a thing worth knowing. Or what an online platform homepage is shouting about, with its bold banners. It is not only a hassle knowing what to buy, but from where. It is so easy to get stuck in a rut, going to the same store for an abundance of 'good' reasons. But the world is your oyster, and the store which best suits you for your dresses might not necessarily be the same for your shirts.

I once asked a sales assistant in Marks and Spencer why their mannequin was so skinny. Her reply was very dry and direct: 'because that's what people want to look like in the clothes'. You know when you are so far beyond insulted, your blinking makes you look like a simpleton? Choosing my battle wisely, I politely but passive-aggressively replied with, 'I don't, but thank you so much', then walked away before anyone got chucked out and banned from the store. The theory is correct for the use of mannequins, of course – so you see how the clothes look – but not necessarily how they will look on you – it is rare a mannequin will reflect the image of the person shopping the look worn. If you are shorter, avoiding regular-fit trousers and ankle-length skirts will do a better job of elongating you. If you have a round core, break it up with a high waist. If you have huge breasts, let those puppies heave – well, my point is: doing what makes you bloody look good *to you* is the key. There isn't one rule we must follow, and we should definitely be wary of projections of a self that will never be.

'I have tried on four pairs of the same size-10 jeans before and they have all varied in cut. I look for cheap "shortcuts" factories take, like not cutting fabric on the warp and weft, which probably means your T-shirt will stretch awkwardly after a few washes.' Sarah, 30 (Designer)

The Ultimate Body

Before we go into the clothes – the best ones, the worst, and the downright fabulous – getting clothes to compliment your body is the key. Whether you're a man or woman or neither, if you have ever struggled with your weight (like me), having that holy grail of a 24-inch waist – or *any* waist – is a feature worth showing off. High waist trousers or jeans are often worn to accentuate the waist, creating an hourglass effect. Yanking up trousers not made for this function can cause an ill fit and actually mask the natural shape of the body, elongate the buttocks and, when done with gusto, shorten the leg length entirely, often shortening the entire body. The point is, if the 1990s sitcom nerd look is desired, go for it – but it would inspire confidence to feel comfortable in clothes that fit (for purpose). When it comes to shirts, if your buttons gape across the chest (or, God forbid, the stomach) invest in a different brand like Thomas Pink, or simply a larger size. Back to the waist – I prefer to dress with a cinched middle, because it gives the illusion of the smaller waist and shapely hips which I wasn't particularly blessed with, the elusive curvaceous figure celebrities have built a career on. However, as sports, cross-fit, flat ripped stomachs and big muscular bums become more and more socially promoted, the range of 'famous' body types have expanded; on social media, you get influencers promoting muscle-solid, 8%-fat hard bodies with solid bums as well as BBL (Brazilian butt-lift) bodies. Don't get me wrong – there is a solid following for the body-positive fuller figure, promoting health at any size, because beauty comes in many shapes and sizes.

I have been an ectomorph most of my life, but since giving birth I have happily crossed over into endomorph territory and have found my home.

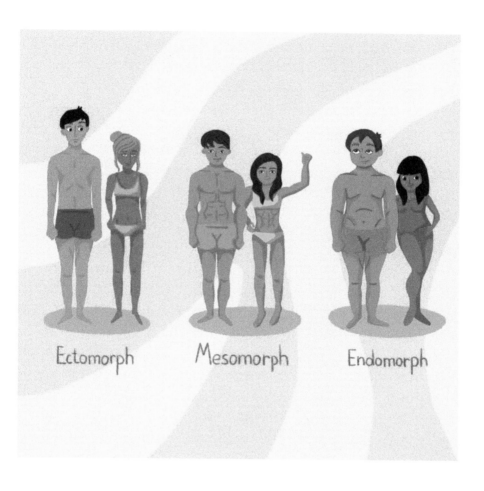

Definitions, both scientific and mine:
Ectomorph / Pencil
Naturally lean and slim
Mesomorph / Pear
Are genetically best equipped to pack on muscle
Endomorph / Apple
Typically have a belly,
usually have a harder time keeping weight off

A healthy diet and exercise are the best recommended advice for a healthy life and a healthy shape, but we were all made different, and boy, does the fashion industry sometimes fail to accommodate for breasts, stomachs, hips and bums. It often also fails to take into account factors such as height, both small and tall, feet, hands, even heads of varying sizes. There are helpful hints on what type of body best suits which types of clothes and accessories in the Appendix, so don't be shy – read on and enjoy shopping (well, obviously) but also getting dressed and feeling great!

New Clothes

By which I mean whatever is considered a new collection in stores at the time of reading this. Going back, there were the strongest, most commercial and internationally known trends in the decades of the past. The sixties were swinging, with miniskirts and military influence, and the seventies were swaying; fabrics in the latter were primarily synthetic, and featured exposed midriffs, flared hems, and platforms. The eighties followed with polyester tracksuits and the like, not very forgiving with the drape. The nineties (yes, what Chris Brown is still wearing these days) were a mixed bag. And in my opinion, no one had a sweeping movement of (dare I call it) 'style' in the noughties. Well – there were the reignited trends of the eighties and nineties, rouge-red hair, K-Fed-style trucker caps and uber-colourful and tattoo-printed clothes alike; hoodies with everything including ball gowns, and who can forget the Kanye West-endorsed shutter shades – style choices or disaster? You decide. The twenty-tens saw a glimmer of hope, with the popularisation of the term 'hipster'; ankles were oh-so in fashion, as were beards and anything vintage. OK, so the ankle thing was a more modern twist on the capris of the sixties. But there was also the integration of the aesthetic I have coined 'looking poor on purpose', popularised by 'designers' like Kanye West. Don't get me wrong, it is no judgement on looking poor – but you know it is a choice when you see a toe poking though limited-edition Converse high-tops. Why? And where are your socks?

Have we run out of ideas? Is originality dead? Well, we are here now – informed shopping is what you need, but by no means stop having fun. Post-2020, with all that has hit the world, you would think fashion would be the last topic on anyone's mind, but alas – the world keeps ticking and Kanye keeps designing. The overriding theme has been comfort – whether that looks like loungewear or four-inch block heels, you do you. It is up to you to make informed decisions when spending that cash money, when you know your shape, and know the clothes that fit it best in the fabrics that work for you, not against you!

'The new wave of twenty-somethings have something to do with the increase in fast fashion reach in the high street.' Rebecca, 27 (Copywriter)

It is not new information that new clothes keep economies all over the world going. Fashion retail is readily available online, across social media, in stores, and via catalogue. The choices are endless. OK, I showed my age with the catalogue line, but trust me – they are still out there.

Red price / Discount

Red price is the opposite of black price. Black price is the RRP of a product, at full recommended retail price. Red price refers to a sale price, discounted price, sometimes known as off-price. When the collection of that season has seen the end of its lifecycle, it may fall into the category of off-price – sometimes sooner if it is a poor seller.

This means the consumer gets a big fat juicy discount when the item is no longer in its prime. Think smaller, more extended periods like Cyber Week (the online and offline aggressive discounting of products, usually the week of Black Friday). Red price season generally occurs twice a year, to conclude the Autumn/Winter season and then the Spring/Summer one. If you are lucky, you may get a midseason sale halfway through to cast off the transitional items which won't carry through the harsh cold or particular trends of winter, or which are too dull, warm and muted for the intensity of summer. Either way, the fashion industry has peaks and troughs when it comes to price points for their customer.

Some brands and retailers choose to take a more spontaneous and reactive approach to their red-price strategy. You could see a 30% discount on a much-loved favourite item in your wish list one day, and the next it will be back to full price. In a contrast to this, the off-price business model has seen lots of success in only retailing red-price fashion, where a good deal can be just as elusive. This is often because it comes at the back end of an article's lifecycle; additionally, you may find popular sizes are in short supply, there aren't many units left in total, or the least popular colourway is all that is left. Often these are campaigns that last but a few days, with a race to buy when the sale goes live. Think mini cyber weeks but every day, at your leisure; a deal a day if you will. In unpredictable economic climates, it is understandable that this business model is booming – but the fact remains that the model exists as a result of overstock in the market. Without this, we would have less waste, reduced textile production, lower impacts on the environment, and less CO_2 emissions. One human's trash is another human's treasure, but in this case, we may be running out of beach to bury it in.

Pre-owned / Second-Hand

Buying and selling clothes second-hand is definitely an area of fashion retail which has increased in mainstream popularity over recent years, increasing the scope of existing business models to venture into this area to increase customer acquisition and retention. It is seen as a sustainable option to buy 'nearly new' fashion, being both business-to-consumer and consumer-to-consumer (B2C and C2C respectively). The old-school bidding site eBay has a long-standing category of fashion resale, but with the big fashion retailers now clawing in old stock for resale it is clear there is a demand for pre-owned clothing. It improves PR, showing that retailers can provide a more sustainable option to the clothing industry and, as with the red-price sites, to reduce overstock by investing less in new goods. The knock-on effect is less waste of materials and water, as well as decreased CO_2 emissions caused from cargo flights. It is not without its downside – there is still the impact of postal mail on the environment maintained, if not increased, as a result of this business model.

What's clear is that the stigma attached to pre-owned goods has drastically decreased during my lifetime. Where hand-me-downs were once frowned upon, or given a raised brow, you are now applauded for showing off your mum's leather blazer or your big brother's oversized Fruit of the Loom jumper. Not only is it a band-aid for the environment, but the aesthetic is also desirable right now. The quality of goods in the second-hand arena is less fast fashion and more mid-range brands, and even luxury if it's in your price range.

Vintage

Calling something vintage depends on the decade it was made in; some companies sell old H&M T-shirts and call them vintage because they are no longer in stores. I'd say that is a miss-sell and should be classified as second-hand. When buying vintage, it is important to ensure it is in good enough nick (condition) for the purpose (getting a few wears out of it before you are bored of it). When I bought two vintage fur coats for five pounds each in the entrance of London's famous Portobello Market from a guy selling them out of a laundry bag and a cardboard box, I thought I'd got a pretty good bargain for the winter. It was dodgy as hell, but I bought them and ran. When I took one to the dry cleaners and he informed me it was real rabbit fur, from the seventies, I lost my nut. Especially when he told me it was a £40 specialist dry-cleaning fee. Instead, I did a free DIY clean (hung it outside for 24 hours after a fabric cleaning spritz), this is the type of recklessness I could afford in my twenties! In my naivety I realised I did not ask the required questions before purchase. My point is, unless it is a similarly happy ending, it is important to know what you are buying, especially if you have reservations, allergies or beliefs which could end in a purchase being a waste of money. This is also the case when it comes to logos, brands, and vintage designers. Having authentication documents for a fifty-year-old designer bag may not always be possible, so doing your due diligence and making sure the seller is reputable will give you the confidence in the authenticity of your purchase.

'I am cheap; after working in the fashion industry for over five years you know how to find the best price for items. If I want an item, I will do everything I can to never pay full price.' Michael, 28 (Fashion Merchandiser)

Jeans

Jeans are made from denim, as you know. But were you aware that the price of denim can be as affordable as less than £5 per yard? And the cost of fixtures and fittings on jeans are miniscule. Bearing this in mind, and the fact that it takes approximately 1.5 yards of 60-inch-wide fabric to make an 'average' sized pair of adult jeans – why aren't all brands sub £10? A denim brand can run on a 60% profit margin, and still make a huge success of themselves. Yes, I left you to do the maths on that one. It is important to factor cost into the thought process when buying a pair of jeans. I'm not stupid; there are of course additional factors, including overheads, staff, machinery, export, import and other logistics. and even expert design which tip a pair over that £10 price point. To buy or not to buy; it is always your prerogative. As a reminder, though, all denim comes from the same cotton-bush plant, whether the material is then chosen to go into the jeans of Primark or those of Versace or Armani. If jeans are 100% cotton there is less flexibility, especially in the hips. 1% elastane is enough to perform a Beyoncé deep squat or dropping it like it's hot in complete comfort. There are varying types of denim: raw or heavily treated for aesthetics; ripping, distressing, waxing and many other techniques are used in the manufacturing process, as well as the use of non-standard fasteners, pocket features, etc. These all contribute to the price and aesthetic of the product itself, and are the determining features which result in the fit and look that have you parting with your hard-earned cash.

A little bit of history: the word *denim* comes from the French *serge de Nîmes*, meaning serge from Nîmes. *Jeans* comes from the French word for the Italian city Genoa (Gênes) where the very first pair was produced. Enough about history – save it for party fashion trivia to impress other unfortunates who haven't read this book. My advice to parents: remind your children when they ask you for money to buy jeans that it's just a bit of cotton, and that they can go to an affordable store for a trendy and inexpensive update.

'Fit is paramount. Longevity of the materials. Obviously if something breaks after one wear, the item goes back but if after one year of wearing my skinny jeans to death, I get a hole in the crotch, I patch it. I know people who buy expensive denim and the same happens.' Sarah, 30 (Designer)

Trousers

Not just for the office these days, trousers come in all different fabrics – natural fabrics like wool or cotton as well as synthetics such as the dreaded viscose. They are available in an abundance of styles: capri, wide-leg, hipster, slim, pleated, elasticated waistband, zip or buttoned. Depending on their use, it is an advantage for trousers to have some level of flexibility in them, especially if they are for work; having a bit of stretch is a useful practical component. On the label's fabric content look for 10% elastane.

Some more history to wow your colleagues and friends: women didn't just go from wearing corsets to box-pleat wide-leg trousers; it has been a gradual transition since the 1800s. Trousers were seldom worn by women until the 1920s, when working women wore trousers, for functionality and practicality. The style icon Katharine Hepburn was a fan of the masculine article of clothing in the 1930s, empowering the choice of clothing for many women.

Today, a pair of trousers are a completely socially acceptable item of clothing for all. An alternative to jeans, trousers can be a more formal option. They also form the second half of a suit; most cuts are available complimentary to the blazer and in the same fabric.

'In the past I could aimlessly wander around the Trafford Centre or Manchester city centre. But after moving to a new country and working for Europe's largest online fashion retailer. I trawl through pictures of similar-looking items and get a number of items delivered to my office. I make my decision whether I like a product within seconds. I rarely look at care labels, and very much go off looks and styles I know already suit me.' Michael, 28 (Fashion Merchandiser)

Dresses

Dresses have now long been established as the highest-selling article in a clothing portfolio for adults, where footwear and handbags once were. Dress shopping is now more similar to an addiction than something to do on a Sunday afternoon whilst watching daytime cookery shows, or, dare I say it, actually visiting the stores on a Saturday. Dresses are a person's best friend, and shopping them is so much more accessible due to the range of online retailers offering discounts, promotions, and permanently low prices on a scary number of options. On a fashion retailer's website that serves women's apparel, this category is often the biggest in terms of options and availability compared to any other clothing category, and much bigger comparatively than the stock that would be carried in a brick-and-mortar store.

Peacocks was a UK company which went into administration in 2012 and was bought by the Edinburgh Woollen Mill Group, after having given birth to seemingly the very first £1.99 dress. In a bid to drive sales in volume, this small range caused quite a stir, not only for its price but what making a dress at that price really meant – for many brands a battle for the lowest prices. Disposable fashion is rife and here to stay. On 13.4.22 I went looking for dresses. On Boohoo.com I found 7,571 dresses, on ASOS 18,086, and on Zalando.de 38,078. Zalando is the largest online retailer in Europe, so this was to be expected – with a 100-day return policy it blows many other retailers out of the water, as well as boasting new innovations such as on-the-spot exchanges and returns by delivery. It's the future. On Zalando, there may be more dresses than women could ever require, including the time to wear them all before the trend fades, but it's so much fun to try, hence the addiction continues.

'I've just learnt what garments will last longer than others and to avoid the super cheap "throwaway" stuff.' Sarah, 30 (Designer)

Affordable fashion now dictates the purchase, use, and disposability of dresses. What with the massive explosion of social media, daily selfies, party pics, shop openings, gigs – what you wear is all over the internet and damn us all if we are seen in the same outfit.

Apple   Pear   Pencil   Hour Glass

Basic Body Shapes and the Best Fit Dresses for Them

Apple – shift / wrap over dress to create a silhouette emphasising a waist-to-hip ratio

Pear – a pencil dress is ideal, wiggle or fitted is key to skim the hips

Pencil – A-line / skater / bubble to accentuate and create a curve on the hips

Hourglass – wear whatever you want!

Skirts

Skirts are cut to so many shapes; their style and relevance is like dresses, but their practicality isn't as sought after, and they aren't as popular as they once were in the 1950s. Cinched in at the waist *Grease*-style, they were once the dress with the conformist label of femininity. To accentuate a waist (above the navel) will generally provide a feminine silhouette, giving the hourglass figure of Jessica Rabbit (there I go with another reference showing my millennial generation). This gives the illusion of a small(er) waist and grabbable hips. Whether the skirt is fitted or A-line, a skirt with a cinched waist can make miracles happen. When it comes to choosing the bottom half of an ensemble, don't forget about the skirt. It can be sexy, sophisticated and downright chic.

'If it's cheap I don't mind if it won't last long.' Rebecca, 27 (Copywriter)

Shorts

Shorts can be defined simply as cut-off trousers. Since Daisy Duke, denim shorts have reigned victorious as the shorts of choice; for festivals, summertime, clubbing, roller-skating, etc. Seemingly with no size bias, no shape or gender is exempt from owning, wearing, and twerking in a pair of denim cut-offs, so make sure you have a staple pair of quality, cause when it moulds to your shape you are sitting pretty! Otherwise, you have other options including high-waisted shorts, knee-length, Bermuda, combat and culottes, to name a few. Often shorts are stored away for summer (which means 13 degrees Celsius and sunny in many a European opinion).

Knitwear

In winter, to keep warm, layer with knitted jumpers and cardigans. You can buy autumn/winter fashion from as early as April (after retailers have bought and launched the trends from the previous Fashion Week). You can buy the new wraps, shawls, knitted skirts, dresses and trousers and the traditional hats, scarves and gloves plus any other new knitted thing off the block. Fabric is an important factor here; 100% wool has pockets of heat to keep out the cold, while 50% wool, 50% polyester can deteriorate in a faster and possibly more unsightly fashion – I'm talking about bobbles, which are a pain in the backside. You need to run a wool setting on your machine, or dare I say it handwash the knits, not forgetting the best practice is to flat-dry them, and you will have a jumper that works for years – good if you paid handsomely for it, even better if you didn't. Every year I used to get a new wool jumper, until I stopped in 2018 because I could no longer find a favourable 100% wool in my go-to store (hence I did not name it). Bummer! Cutting corners loses customers.

'I became a designer originally because I always had a specific way that I wanted something to look and could never find it. I was always making my own clothes rather than settling for something not quite right.' Sarah, 30 (Designer)

Shirts

Shirts made from 100% cotton are ideal for indoor office jobs, anywhere around 8 hours of working a day. Cotton breathes, and it's durable and looks fabulous in crisp white, too. The thing to bear in mind is the shape. Brands often charge a higher retail price due to the pattern and cut, to mould to the contours of the body. If you are provided with a polyester uniform, handing it back to your boss with the suggestion of having a fabric preference isn't usually possible, so it is advisable to wear a barrier of a vest or tee between the flesh and the poly fabric.

People generally have curves, and shirts need to accommodate them. It is not so attractive to have buttons stretching beyond what's reasonable at the chest, nor buttons popping open at the navel when you sit down after lunch. Shirt companies like Thomas Pink or Burberry do it best, in my opinion, but it can be a lottery looking for work shirts on the high street that can last the test of time, cuff to collar; it can be necessary, though, as if there's one thing you should always try on before you buy, it's a work shirt. If you find your brand, I'd suggest you stick to it.

The label in this case won't help you find a well-fitting shirt, but something you can look out for is good seam work. Buttons, as previously suggested, shouldn't look like they are repelled by the hole when fastened i.e., loose and ill-fitting once fastened. A fitted (two-finger gap) collar. Please, no pirate sleeves – Jack Sparrow has no place giving style advice. After all of that it should fit your body, and be a flattering length, stopping at least below the belt buckle.

Sportswear

The function of sportswear is traditionally for use during exercise. Although for some this is something of a dirty word, for others it is a way of life, and sportswear is worn not only in the gym, but, for those for whom the streets are their gymnasium, as part of their everyday attire. We all know the stereotype yummy mummies dressed in a seven-day-a-week uniform of varying athleisure options. An inspirational person said to me in 2016 that jogging tights were the new jeans. I guess in a way, that predicted the athleisure uniform worn by many today. Sportswear has transitioned from functional to trend-led fashion. It isn't really a surprise; often sportswear provides the service to suck it all in and hold it all still. A clear advantage whether you are running through the concrete jungle or popping along to informal drinks.

A commercial socially acceptable piece of clothing now includes leggings. Last famous in the eighties, with icons such as Kelly Kapowski and Lisa Turtle (of *Saved by the Bell* fame), they were often accompanied by oversized jumpers and large tops hanging off the shoulder. In this day and age, they're often paired with a slogan or brand down the leg. Brands like Nike and Adidas have led the way in fashion tech for function. Heat tech allows for efficient cooling whilst physically exerting yourself as well as withstanding the colder climates. Genius. It's also a super-stretchy fabric which shapes your body into a smooth, alluring form.

Look @ the Size Labels

It isn't enough to shop for your size by looking at the label or tag; knowing your size in reference to the region you are buying from is also a contributing factor to ensuring a purchase is made with confidence. International fashion is open to us all, thanks to the internet, but it is a fact that sizes and ways of designating them vary widely between countries. Knowing your size in relation to the country of design as well as the brand itself is very important. There are size charts to help you on your way, but they don't take into account the fact that your EU size 38 may cut off circulation in one brand and gape in another. Sizing has become a guide, especially as the people of the world are growing – we have never been as tall or wide as we are today as a species, and sizes must adapt with this growing trend (pun intended).

Sizes have changed from thirty-five years ago when my mum was my age, already with seven kids under her belt and looking trim and fabulous. When I 'borrowed' her clothes in my twenties (can't call them vintage if she's still wearing them) the size on them said 14 or 16, but they fit me despite the fact that I was a 10 or 12. Sizes have got bigger to cope with the growing Brits. It is a well-documented fact that the notoriously voluptuous size 12 Marilyn Monroe would be the equivalent of a size 8 today.

Marilyn Monroe photographed by Philippe Halsman for LIFE
magazine in 1952. I bet you wish you had tickets to that gun show.

**'For beautiful shop windows, see KaDeWe or Zara. They also
do a lot of in-house events with specific mottos, combine more and
more different "areas", and present themselves as lifestyle stores,
offering books, headphones, and interior items next to their
clothes rack, while brewing fresh coffee for the customer. It's all
about engaging multiple senses and cross-innovation.' Anna,
(Strategic Marketing & Performance Manager)**

With all the information above, just remember, take brand, time,
and meals ingested into consideration when shopping. Shopping on a
full stomach can manage expectations further down the line, when
you want something to wear after that mocha you drank which quite
definitely was not lactose free. If you shop during a three-day detox

cleanse, you might end up with something you may never fit into again. I am officially a UK size 10-16 depending where I shop, but I am OK with that, because the only thing the clothes have in common is that they fit me. Clothes should look amazing on you; to reiterate, the clothes should be the focus, not the number printed on the label. To save time have a look through your wardrobe and see which brands fit the best and take note of the size printed within them. These days, shopping online gives you sizing advice based on the brand and your previous purchases, this is not only to prevent excessive returns but also to increase customer satisfaction. Online shopping has its advantages, and the use of AI for personalisation is for sure one of them.

Look @ the Suit Labels

A suit can be a corporate professional's second skin. It generally comprises a blazer or suit jacket on top, and, to cover the essentials, a skirt or trousers below, all of which are cut from the same cloth. The suit originated in Britain, and is typical formal attire in Western culture.

Though usually a two-piece, a business suit may also come as a three-piece, incorporating the addition of a waistcoat, for the more style-conscious person with an attention to detail.

Dinner suits and tuxedos are appropriate for highly formal black-tie events. The dinner jacket (the US term) sometimes just refers to a blazer, which in some social establishments you cannot be granted access without. Tuxedos are for formal occasions, affairs which should be treated with the utmost respect. Given the nature of events where a tuxedo is required, 100% polyester isn't the best investment. Typically, a tuxedo has satin for the lapels and on the outside seam of the trouser legs – pure luxe.

'I wear down the crotch in jeans quite quickly so tend to not buy super-expensive jeans, but I do go mid-range due to finding the fit better if you pay a bit more money. I am willing to spend more money if it's a basic piece that can last years and will go with anything. Or items such as tuxedos.' Michael, 28 (Fashion Merchandiser)

Looking at the labels within a suit is not so simple – there are several layers of fabric, types of stitch and other detailing, and multiple styles to choose from.

When shopping for suits there are four options:

- A custom-made suit is completely one of a kind. Produced from a block of the customer, where a pattern is made for the suit of choice.

- A made-to-measure suit is made from a pre-existing pattern, amended to fit the customer, still on a limited basis.

- Off-the-rail is from the brand's standardized sizes, which can be tailored to fit the customer.

- Separates, where each article (top, bottom, waistcoat) is sold separately to get the best fit.

Special Washing Instructions – Suits

Especially important because of the fabric of the suit, it is important to follow the cleaning instructions to maintain the longevity, quality, and integrity of the suit. Many people have suits for years, even decades. If this sounds like you, it is more than likely going to be a dry-clean-only affair.

Look @ the Coat Labels

Coats are, for all intents and purposes, a barrier between you and the cold as much as they can be the biggest exterior fashion statement. Its purpose is important for the environment you are in. Unlike my introduction to the harsh winters of Berlin – which can go to -10°C in January – the average temperatures of London see 5°C, New York 2°C and Rome 8°C. The question of whether a coat is fit for purpose was one I never thought needed depth or context until moving to Germany. That's not to say you have to cover yourself in multiple plastic binbags to keep in the heat. There are plenty of outerwear options which don't all look like you are hiking through Saxony.

When dealing with the effects of global warming, increasing the likelihood of temperatures dropping below zero in winter, it is very important to check that label; more often than not the fabric composition is the key to unlocking the truth behind whether the coat is the right one for you against the price tag demanded of it.

'Coats are my thing and Zara seems to get it right every season.' Angela, 50 (Fashion Buying Assistant)

The style of coat is completely dependent on you, but if you get cold legs and enjoy the look you may want to consider investing in full-length. Likewise, if you find the additional material bothersome in a full-length, go for a ¾ length, mid, or short coat. Jackets are defined as simply an outer garment which extends to the waist or hips, with a fastening and sleeves – in other words a short coat. Jackets, to the average Jane or Joe, are more commonly referred to as lightweight items of outerwear, but strictly it should just be a reference to length.

Look at the label and see what fabrics are used. If it is mixed with plastic fabrics, it inhibits the breathability of the article, and the warmth incurred is a product of dense non-airing polymers. The wool percentage in coats is like gold. Wool can be tricky; although it is a warm natural fibre, it is also the trigger for many people's allergies. It is, however, a superior fabric for making coats, clothes, knitwear, and accessories. There are also jackets stuffed with feathers, again from both natural and synthetic origins. Down (from ducks and geese) is a popular higher-priced option of feather to stuff a winter coat or puffer, as down is the soft layer of feathers closest to a bird's skin, which do not have quills. If you want to make a purchase on sale, a quick quality check on a coat filled with cheaper feathers are the quills or calamus poking out through the stitching. This is easier seen in store, where the item has been out for a bit longer, received a few try-ons and maybe shows some wear and tear.

Is it waterproof? Often the label provides some sort of identification of whether the outer layer can resist penetration of water. Wax on the outer layer can provide a barrier between the wearer and rain and snow, keeping you warm and dry within. Mass production of wax jackets started around the eighteenth century, and brands such as Barbour (established in 1894) and Belstaff are leaders in the waxed canvas outerwear game.

The lining and pockets – the integrity here might degrade long before you even get a chance to put the coat in the laundry and ruin the thing. I have on one unsavoury occasion put my travel card and keys in my new full-length Zara coat only for them to fall through and land by my ankles. Rummaging in my coat and pulling out only used tissues to present to the bus driver was not only shocking, but also meant I was that girl that delayed the London bus. Shame.

Look at the fasteners – look for a YKK or the brand's logo if it's a zip. If poppers, look at the stitch detail – my experience with poppers has been tragic, but that's no reason to give up completely; they're best implemented as a second fastener to a zip. Buttons are a traditional fastener to a wool or poly-blend coat, but again, check the stitch, turn the coat to look inside and see how close and tight the stitch is.

These are references for an investment buy, something you would like to wear, use, and enjoy for many seasons to come.

Special Washing Instructions – Coats

Most machines these days have settings for wool, fine wool, quick wash, cold wash – and at different temperatures. Leather cannot be put in the washing machine. I feel like this is an obvious but necessary piece of information that should possibly have been given somewhat earlier in this guide, but better late than never. Other than leather, if there isn't a setting on the machine for your fabric, pop along to the dry cleaners; they provide a service.

'Also, I have my favourite brands: Whistles, for that fab dress; Joseph for the ultimate well-cut trouser that I have had in my wardrobe for the last fifteen years and is still good as new, and a sexy fit for my body; Malene Birger, for bling tops; Zara fort shirts and coats. If I need a treat, I love Marni for the simplicity, unique style, and minimalist look.' Angela, 50 (Fashion Buying Assistant)

Look @ the Lingerie Labels

Underwear comes before everything, and is the starting point of the barrier which protects your body from the outside elements. One of the leaders in the UK, more for functionality and with a splash of fashionability in underwear, is Marks & Spencer. For goodness' sake – the Queen of England got her underwear from M&S, one of the UK's oldest companies, established in 1884. The scientific research and ethical manufacture which goes into a pair of underpants makes for longer lasting, comfortable and sexy underwear, which can compensate for the price points being higher than that of some of its competitors.

Bras

It might be surprising to hear that if you're wearing two to three bras consistently then they require replacement after around six months. This was thought to be a myth by many friends and family, but ask any sales consultant in a lingerie speciality store and they will confirm. The lace, elastane, and construction of the bra will wear through in half a year or so. Try it yourself – take an older bra and compare it to the same bra but brand new, recently sized to fit, and see the difference. Challenge accepted? I'll be accepting thank you gifts.

It is also a part of life that our bra size will fluctuate during the years, even during the month. Annual sizing (at least) would be of benefit, to ensure your baps are getting exactly what they need.

Sports Bra

The same goes for sports bras, but even more so if you think about it; the primary function in a sports bra is to reduce movement against gravity itself plus the additional force of movement when running, cross-fit training, or during any kind of vigorous stretch routine that attempts to force your breasts south, east, or west. This is especially true if losing weight; the skin will be trying to shrink back, but letting your breasts swing around your neck with every lap of the racing track won't help stretch marks or skin elasticity.

Briefs

I buy my pants the same place as the Queen of England. Marks & Spencer. 95% cotton, 5% elastane black high bikini brief beauties. I live in them – renewed with five-pack every six months. Having a 100% cotton gusset is mandatory. A gusset is the piece of material sewn into a garment to strengthen or enlarge a part of it, which in this case is the bit which covers your sensitive parts. The price of cotton briefs varies considerably, from budget Primark to M&S to Calvin Klein, which is still cotton, but damn fine cotton. In these three cases, you are paying for the cotton, the cut, and the brand respectively. No one wants an ill-fitting, parachute-like pair of briefs, because if you ever get caught with your trousers down, so to speak, you want to at least have a decent pair of pants on. Don't bare any more shame than you must.

Lace Lingerie

Lace is a beautiful fabric, which I didn't cover previously in the fabrics chapter because it fits better down here (something you may also wish to say about your underwear). Lace is often made from polyamide, and frequently mixed with elastane for ease of movement. It is often used as a trim on tops and skirts – all-over lace on outerwear (as opposed to underwear) is a trend which comes in and out of fashion but will always be risky, owing to the fact that it is translucent at best. Wear what feels good, but if you're asked for your hourly rate, think of something smart to reply to the fool and keep it moving. A person's body needn't be an invitation for commentary, no matter what you're wearing.

Special Washing Instructions – Lace Lingerie

For maximum integrity of the lace article, it should not be machine washable, but should be hand-washed with like colours for best results. To be even more specific, you should use lukewarm water, with non-biological soap or powder, making sure to give all relevant areas a good hearty clean. Air drying is also preferential, to reduce some of the effects which prevent items from looking fresh, like the slight stretching which occurs when moisture leaves the garment on the heater.

Look @ the Accessories

Accessories are used not only to dress up an outfit but also to simplify it, and they can make or break that outfit. High-street stores and fashion houses may refer to the entire accessories collection with the umbrella term 'non-clothing'. This includes footwear, handbags, even umbrellas themselves, as well as jewellery and what are referred to as 'soft accessories', a category which incorporates hats, gloves, scarves, headbands and wraps. Hosiery may also be within this category, as well as socks, leggings, and leg warmers.

Soft Accessories

Hats, gloves and scarves are made of a variety of fabrics, many of which have been covered in previous chapters. Investment pieces are made from the wool of animals like sheep and goats, but are subject to wear and degradation. Not pretty when your very expensive angora scarf is brought out of storage only to have moth-eaten pea-sized holes it didn't have the winter before. It is the nature of the beast. Synthetics are affordable and take to dyes, and you can often get matching sets at affordable prices whilst you are there for the ultimate Christmas gift: one for them and one for yourself – why not!

Hard Accessories

There's no such thing – just to clarify in case you get caught in a fashion chat and someone who thinks they are clever and refers to the new 'hard accessories' on the market. You can be like 'damn, love, read a book!'

Hats

When shopping for a hat, functionality is paramount. Baseball caps are traditionally made from wool, but mass-produced options are more commonly made in cotton and cotton-synthetic mixes. Look to the snapback to assess the quality; if a cheap, super-bendy plastic has been used, I'd steer clear, as they can be an indication of counterfeit items. Caps can also be made by size, without the adjustable strap; these are generally more expensive but give an improved fit.

Felt is often used as an alternative to wool, which is desirable for its warmth, durability, and protection. It is a fabric often used for trilbies. A stiffener is often required to maintain its shape, but it is also a commonly used fabric for the more elaborate floppy hat. Any full-brimmed hat for winter is best in wool, so bargains which can be had on the high street should be snapped up quick, fast, and in a hurry.

Whether it is a cap, trilby, fishermen, or flat cap, a leather hat is a symbol of cool. And don't you forget it, Samuel L. Jackson has proved it on more than one occasion. Of course, a hat made from polyurethane (PU) can supply you with the same aesthetic at a fraction of the price, but the point is the same. If you would like to go out of your way to increase the heat at the top of your head as a student of style, you can do so – but by all means, know if the cost outweighs the sense by checking it is really leather first. Can you look this cool?

Samuel L. Jackson

Gloves

Gloves are a simple beast: they keep your hands warm. Not much to ask for, right? To prevent a sweaty palm and wrinkly fingers, a glove produced from a natural / animal fibre is the best you can do for your skin. If you find the single layer of wool insufficient, you can (either at a premium or sub-£10 these days) purchase leather gloves with a natural lining.

Gloves, mittens and muffs are ideal for keeping your phalanges from freezing, tips to wrists. However, trying to pay for your coffee, get out your travel card or, more importantly, use your phone can be unmanageable in traditional gloves. Touchscreen gloves are one of the most successful inventions using tech in the fashion industry incorporating fashion and function. In a world where you can't go five minutes without picking up your phone and checking your Twitter, Facebook or Instagram, let alone the rest – you can do it all comfortably with your gloves on.

Belts

Belts are a functional item and are not always appreciated as a fashion accessory. One would rather see a bit of leather strapped around the waist than the underwear or ass crack of a perfect stranger, and that's when these long strips of fabric become as useful as a harness on a mountain climb.

Other options for keeping your trousers up where they are supposed to sit are suspenders or braces. The main component in these is elastane – fundamental to keeping the levels of comfort whilst holstering your trousers up at your waist, in addition to providing the functionality of one size fits all.

Sunglasses

I have always liked what I liked. So, this is just a guide: try as many shapes on as possible and see what 'fits'. A large list of styles can be found in the appendix. It is strongly recommended to suit the shape of your face to the frames, but it isn't like fitting a shirt. Different brands cater to different head sizes, let alone shapes, so I recommend wearing what makes you feel fabulous when you put them on. When I was living in Milan, with many more sunny days than London, the necessity for sunglasses was as high as a pair of black leggings on a fat day; it provides protection and security.

Whether aviator, round, or cat's eye, there are so many shapes of sunglasses to choose from. I have a heart-shaped face (a well-rounded heart at that, as my cheeks are undeniably plump). The general rule is, if a pair of sunglasses are angular and you have a round face, go crazy, and vice versa. My rule is to wear what makes you feel like tabletop dancing, and own it!

Hosiery

Hosiery is generally made from nylon with elastane; there isn't any getting away from it. However, the variety of shades we can get has never been as broad as it is today. Going for wool or cotton blend tights is definitely a choice for the winter months, with a stricter choice of colours available (what I am trying to say is don't expect to get a skin-colour match here). On top of the colour of the tights, another consideration is the denier. Visually the thicker the tights the higher the denier. Anything above 40 can substitute for a sleeker look than a pair of wool thigh-highs. The higher the denier, the stronger, thicker, more opaque and more durable a pair of hosiery will be. The aesthetic of lighter deniers (5 to 30) is a more sheer appearance, with a much lighter fabric – but damn it as a result they are more susceptible to runs and snags, damage in general detracting from their near-naked leg appeal.

There is also the option to go for aesthetics, and choose hosiery with fishnets and other more intricate designs built into the fabric – here a higher denier (80+) is recommended for longevity.

1. Do not settle for a shade of hosiery that makes you look like you borrowed a pair of mannequin legs for the day.

2. Do your research – don't pay a small mortgage just because they do 200 shades. Ask forums, speak to friends, and look around. It is only nylon at the end of the day.

3. Ensure the denier is appropriate for the function.

Socks

Might not seem a major concern, but think about it – from the time you put your foot into a shoe at the start of your day to the moment you remove it in the evening, you could have a twelve-hour slog of a sock–shoe combination. Cotton socks are therefore the most desirable option for maximum foot hygiene. There is often 10% elastane to factor in for freedom of movement. Avoid polyester socks for long expeditions and sports. It's a bit obvious, but a healthy recommendation nonetheless.

Look @ the Bag

This chapter could go on forever. Buying a handbag should be a well-thought-out decision with a clear budget and function in mind before even attempting to log into your app or cross the threshold of that store. Handbags take the brunt of everyday life, whether you commute to the office, take care of the household or live a carefree life of socialising.

The function is paramount. If the bag is for nappies, it should be fit for purpose. Yes, designer brands make baby bags, so there is no need to use your Louis Vuitton shopper for this purpose. Likewise, if all you carry is a purse and a smile, trade down to a smaller crossover or shoulder bag. There is no need to use a leather holdall for the gym; when everything gym-related is damp, not ideal for leather. This is more preaching to the choir here, I know. Things to consider:

- The materials. Many designer brands use synthetic fabrics in bags; despite their high price tag, the handles are usually the first to 'crack', leaving this bag aesthetically ugly. The longevity required for the bag is often a factor playing into the purchase; if you see wear in the handle whilst testing out the bag, it will likely only get worse. Look at how the handle creases not only on the part handled, but also on the fixture from the body of the bag. Look to see if the integrity looks fit for purpose: if you travel light, it may be just fine for the fashion season it is bought for; if you're looking for something lasting a bit longer, a natural fibre overall would be a better bet.

- Bags can transfer colour onto your clothes. Look for a warning label which MUST be attached – if not, you can claim a full refund. It does go the other way; you don't want your indigo jeans to transfer blue dye onto your fabulous new white handbag.

- Look at the edge paint (where the bag has been stitched together) – sometimes this is done inaccurately in the factory, which can make the bag look cheap. This can happen to all retailers.

- If there is a brand logo, check that the letters are screwed on straight. Again, all retailers, high and low end, are guilty of this. It only takes one wonky MK for people to start talking about quality issues or falling off the back of the truck.

- Inside pockets. Is the bag worth its price? Do you get inside storage for your mobile phone, secret storage for hygiene products? Is it fit for purpose?

- The design. Bags can be decorated with beading, tassels, or sewn-on adornments. Do the stitching and fixings look secure? If in store, look at the floor – have any fallen off since the shop opened that morning?

- Fasteners – as previous. Does the zip work? That is a good place to start. Is the magnet in the popper strong enough to keep the bag closed?

- Try the bag out – put it on your shoulder, back, across your body or in your hand. Walk around with it, feel secure that it can integrate itself into your life with ease, as if it has always been there. Make all the adjustments on the straps, cords, opening and closing compartments. Once you are happy with it, go to the checkout felling fully confident with your purchase. Only the bank can make bag shopping a heinous experience, so enjoy!

Look @ the Jewellery Labels

Jewellery doesn't come with labels per se. When shopping at a jeweller, there are specific markings which explain the carat of gold, or whether it's sterling silver, etc. I won't go into that level of detail because it is not my forté – the jeweller, unless a crook, will inform you about that very important purchase. But here are some basics.

Gold

Gold is a precious metal, but in excess has either a Flavor Flav or J.Lo 'Love Don't Cost a Thing' look; it depends how you carry it off. Yellow gold is popular in Asian cultures, compared with the paler gold more commonly seen in Western cultures. As gold is an element with very low reactivity, gold of 9 karat and up should never change colour and go green, so if it does, please revert to the salesperson and demand all your money back and a full apology. Let's go back to the basics. A karat is a unit of measurement to define, as alluded to above, how many parts of gold are present in the alloy of 24 parts (meaning 9 karat gold is 9/24). The smaller the amount of gold, the higher the potential for the final alloy to react and cause unsightly consequences like skin discolouration. The higher the mix of gold the more durable and long-lasting the piece of jewellery. For a wedding ring go for a high karat – don't take shortcuts here, because if that marriage is for forever, the rings should be made to last the course.

Silver

Silver has had a big revival since 2013. Its use in multiwear (wearing multiple pieces of similar jewellery, like rings) has seen its popularity soar. Again, if it is sterling silver then it should not change the colour of your skin under any circumstances. The most common silver available in your drug store is S925, which means it is 925 parts silver per 1,000. For more pure silver, anywhere from 92.5% above will give you a higher mix of silver; at 99.9% it is often referred to as fine silver. Having a lower share of alloy metals such as copper or nickel reduces the risk of tarnishing.

Costume Jewellery

Costume jewellery often comes unmarked due to components being manmade. It's made for fashion, but don't get too attached to it because as fast as it came into your life it can leave – or at least a synthetic gemstone can; whether link or clasp, its shelf life is defined by its use. My advice, if you love it buy two, and the sadness of its missing stones and broken pendants won't be as tragic.

Look @ the Footwear Labels

I was turned into a shoe snob at a very early age – five, in fact – when my dad explained the beauty of a pair of leather shoes and all the different types of shoes there are for different occasions. He taught me that it is OK to own many pairs of shoes as long as their end use is varied. Now I stand proud at 200 pairs, which may sound excessive, especially when you compare it to my husband who proudly owns four. What can I say?

Either on the sole or stuck inside the shoe you should find the composition of the construction. Below is a key to some of the symbols you may have seen and what they all mean. From the day I learnt this, I was hooked on shoes. My dad broke it all down when he bought me my school uniform shoes from Shelly's London. My school shoes were previously bought by my mother, who now was busy taking care of her other six children and working as a chef. They were green (from that day my favourite colour), burnished, lace-up wingtip brogue derbys. One of the best days of my life!

Here is the key for your reference.

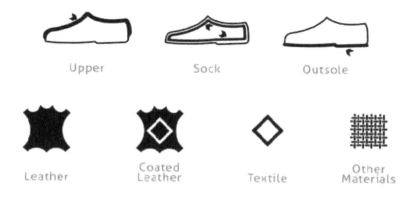

| Upper | Sock | Outsole |

| Leather | Coated Leather | Textile | Other Materials |

Upper

The upper is the exterior material used for making the shoe. You can get shoes in leather, PU, textile and other fabrics – but also a mix of any of the above. I have gone into detail about leather in its section of the chapter on fabrics. There is little it doesn't do in a pair of shoes. Insulating, adapting to the shape of your feet, and it's durable and water resistant. You cannot beat a solid pair of leather shoes, both upper and sock as above.

Textile is used heavily in sports footwear, but can often be mixed with other more hardwearing fabrics for aesthetics, like tweed or canvas mix on leather or PU shoes.

Fast fashion favours polyurethane (PU) for the manufacture of easy-come easy-go footwear in all guises for men, women, and children. The investment you put into your shoes generally determines what you get out of them. However, there are blogs and websites dedicated to the theory of high-end expensive designer shoes not lasting long enough to tell a tale. Personal experience is one thing, and an opinion endorsed by a noted writer is another. My advice is if you can, do. If you have the money, use it as you wish. Don't go around walking on eggshells in your Louboutins, as nothing lasts forever. Whether they last as long as your Topshop pumps or longer, enjoy them whilst they are on your feet – making you feel like your most fabulous self.

Sock / Lining

This can also be made from leather in many high-end retail brands; sometimes pig leather is used, as it is cheaper but still with many of the same desirable characteristics as calf leather. If it's pig leather, you can tell by the pocks in the skin. PU can also be used for lining to save costs, savings which sometimes are transferred to the customer for a more affordable retail price.

Sole

Soles can be made from leather as well, but the weight of an entire human body pounding the pavement regularly enough can result in erosion of the sole. In fact, to use leather depreciates the sole a lot faster than if it was made of plastic. In this case its end use is more suited to a shoe which gets a lot of wear out of it.

There is an extensive glossary of knowledge covered in the back – because bunions are no one's best friend. Let's try our hardest to keep them away now, shall we.

'I started my career as a product developer, and I learnt a lot about footwear construction and communication with factories.' Sarah, 30 (Designer)

Trainers

Trainers are traditionally fit for the purpose of running, cross training, aerobics, dancing or basketball. However, aesthetics and brand have overshadowed necessity, and fashion and trends have taken the wheel. Whether they are endorsed by a famous basketballer, or made for the purpose of running the hell out of some red tarmac, trainers have become the comfort footwear of choice.

Leaders in the field Adidas and Puma, originally founded by a pair of German brothers, have a sixty-plus-year history in sports-shoe manufacturing. Nike are obviously the US giants. Other companies whose technology stems from the science are brands like New Balance, whose founder used a chicken's balance as inspiration to improve performance in posture and stability.

'On some things, like trainers, I will try my size on somewhere and then go online to get them the cheapest.' Sarah, 30 (Designer)

Look @ the Brand Tags

We have come a long way from the plastic kimball / price tag / brand label, which leaves a gaping hole and destroys the garment when punched through the fabric. A cheap tag is usually a white plastic kimball attached to white printed paper. A more deluxe brand might choose to use cord or braided rope looped through the tag. The more expensive cords are thicker, waxed even, and connected in a knot or plastic fixing. Don't even get me started on the tag itself, which can be made from paper of many weights and qualities, plastic – even textile, with the brand logo printed, sewn, or embossed onto it.

The type of tag to use is a big consideration for a brand, as it is often a representation of the DNA of that brand. An investment in a good tag usually correlates with a fashion collection of calibre.

'My shopping preferences depend on where I'm living. When I'm in Jamaica I tend to shop online more. In the States, I would say it's an even mix between the two. In Berlin, I shop almost exclusively in stores. But wherever I shop, I approach it like a sport.' Shoshannah, 28 (Student)

Without boring you, here are some examples from my own purchases – a mixture of paper, coated materials and plastic, attached to the garment by woven cord or cheap plastic already banished to the recycling bin.

93

Look @ the Price Tags

Not just a song by Jessie J, the price tag can be the final point of realisation for many a purchase. Will it go home with you or not? Make or break, fight or flight! The price tag can be the best or worst part of a shopping trip.

Currency Conversions

Unless like me you like your mental arithmetic, having the RRPs of other markets on the label may be inconsequential. However, working in fashion for international brands, I am a frequent user of currency conversions. Especially since leaving the UK and living and working in Europe, I have noticed that the price of a litre of milk or a pack of broccoli can be wildly different when converting into pounds sterling. I'm just saying – 49p in London, €1.99 in Berlin – what's up with that? It goes beyond the supermarket, of course; and back to fashion – brands selling internationally can often give RRPs based on calculations to provide a median for the fluctuation in conversions throughout the year.

'I definitely price compare – between the States and Europe mostly.' Shoshannah, 28 (Student)

Some stores don't give the best deal on price. It could be that the store is based in the UK, including its distribution centers (or DCs), and sells outside the UK; the logistical costs to get to the flagship LA store are far greater than getting a delivery to the London flagship.

Online companies are not exempt from this. Unless you are savvy some retailers can ship to all their markets on competitively fast delivery times which can incur higher costs. I digress. The point is that brands operating from a particular country may provide the best value when converted to other currencies from around the world.

Look @ the Websites

Websites and online stores come primarily in two formats, desktop or mobile, but in general the difference between a budget site and a high-investment shop can be seen in a few ways. There is no definite correlation between the shop's online presence and the quality of the goods – some stores are simply unwilling to invest in the shop if the product speaks for itself. Having a good UI (user interface) is mandatory; having icons for shopping, size preferences and adding to basket are mandatory. Having multi-language options is an advantage to an international site; not only may you want to shop in another language, but also to shop when in a different country and sign in to the local domain.

Depending on the size of the store, where there might be tens of thousands of products available on any given day, a retailer should always have accessible filters on the home page to reduce the amount of content you need to sift through. Being able to select preferences when you log in is also a desirable feature, as is having some sort of 'favourite' system, to bookmark things you have not yet made up your mind about, like when you pick something off the rack and walk around the store with it over your arm until you decide if you want to buy it or not. As you don't have the luxury of a mannequin on which to build and suggest looks on the journey, there should be images of models and outfits. Having models is an investment –if the main images on the website are clothes floating on an invisible body, a lower investment was made into selling the products online. The brand's job is to inspire you to purchase, and an online presence is no different – if you're not feeling inspired, find a different .com.

Look @ the Online Details

Due to the complete absence of a store assistant to gather more information the content on websites at the article level should be as clear as possible. It will never fully replace the physical shopping experience, but should make up for it with convenience and speed. You should get every detail, even the ones you take for granted in a store, accessible via a drop-down, scroll, or ungrouping a field. The experience of leaving the house to go shopping should be virtually replicated, sparing only the details of transport (when will telepods be invented, already?).

'I shop online for speed; I see it, I buy it.' Angela, 50 (Fashion Buying Assistant)

We are in a technology age, in which shopping online is a common fact of life; therefore, the user-friendly, navigational functionality of a website, compatible with all desktops, mobiles, and tablets, should be as necessary as the website in the first place. Websites should have a good user experience, with easy-to-access steering. Often filters are used to select and isolate the requirements, including size, colour, price, brand, category, fit, length, etc. Important pieces of information like composition, fastener, washing / care instructions and fitting or sizing guides should always be available, as well as clear details about the measurements of the model and the size they are wearing.

'My choice of career hugely affects the way I shop in many ways. I remember a lecture at uni where the lecturer told us about a book called _Why We Shop_, which was the science of shopping. I read it eagerly and the rest is history.' Sarah, 30 (Designer)

When picking up a new pair of jeans, as the previous ones have finally sprung a perfectly placed hole between your thighs (which may cause embarrassment at the weekend away you scheduled to meet the parents of your other half), you need to have all the pieces of information you would normally have if you were shopping in a brick-and-mortar store available to you. (It went great by the way.) Back to online: you should, as mentioned in the previous chapter, pick up the item and check that you can wash and dry it by your regular means at home. Check that it is made in a country you're happy with, that the fastener is screwed on tight; if a zip (preferably YKK), or if it's an old-school button fly, that they are sewn on / punched in securely. Also check the type of fabric: if denim is distressed, will it disintegrate in a year? Does it have 10% elastane for that welcome stretch and pull with everyday movement? There are also the other things, like leg length – if you don't know your own, buy a couple of options and find out. Few are as unlucky as me to be a 33-inch leg, when they generally come in 32 and 34.

'I mostly shop online as I'm limited by time, being at work during the week, and I don't want to spend my weekends in the city shopping. I normally spend half an hour during my lunch hour perhaps once a month checking out my usual reliable brand to have a browse, i.e., Topshop, Zara, ASOS. These are my go-to places because of their variety and the frequency with which they change their ranges; each time I go back there is something new.' Sarah, 30 (Designer)

Key Online Companies

Zalando is Europe's leading ECOM retail fashion site (and my current employer). No bias to say they have shot to fame and produced intimidating numbers, like a €14.3 billion gross turnover in 2021, +34% growth on the previous year in sales after being established fourteen years previously in 2008. There are companies who have been running for decades and haven't achieved figures like this. At the top of their priorities for brand DNA is customer satisfaction, high availability, customer-centric marketing and planning, all directed towards customer acquisition and customer loyalty.

eBay is a bidding-style website which allows more freedom for sellers to divulge information about the product they are selling. However, withholding information reduces the chances of a sale online as this is the only source of data. eBay is the leading bidding website in just about every category, including fashion.

Amazon, the retailer and marketplace, the legend. They have propelled themselves into first place for online retail companies. The site is open to private sellers and Amazon wholesale. In 2021 in the USA, there were 151.9 million Amazon Prime customers, getting perks like free and expedited delivery, amongst other advantages that are product-specific. This ranges from fashion to electrical goods.

ASOS sells their own branded fashion as well as other international brands. It has a magnificent amount of choice in nearly every product category of fashion, clothing and accessories. Their humble beginnings are testament to a winning business model. The website is simple to navigate, and information is easy to find, but it is the information which isn't on the product page you need to be wary of. It's like the fine print on a hidden label hanging off an item in store. It could be dry-clean only, colour transfer, or even 100% viscose.

Online Product Ratings

How do websites know how their product is functioning if customers don't review it? Websites rely on product-rating features to gather information about their customer service, layout and advertising. It can also influence their order quantities of certain products and brands in the future. Items which cannot be returned, like briefs, could be the highest-selling item from a department store, but the seams might fall apart after a few washes. I can't imagine many people are going to strut into Selfridges to complain about a faulty batch of underwear and present their evidence... eek. The weight of customers' opinion and experience can even influence the brand's strategy, and is therefore invaluable. So, next time, consider how your thoughts can influence the brands you know and love, fashion for thought.

Bounce rates, click-throughs, views and visibility are all great key performance indicators, but if someone reports that their new T-shirt was just too big around the neckline, it is more informative than a return with the broad reason 'too big'. It also favours a deeper buy-in to an article for next year, month, or immediate replenishment.

Service is also improved with honest feedback. I urge everyone, if you have time, to leave reviews – the only way things will improve is if you let brands know what their successes and failures are. Honesty is great, as is constructive feedback, but trolls beware – make the feedback useful, or save your time and polish your horns instead.

'I don't tend to rate. Unless prompted, or unless I need to, like with eBay.' Rebecca, 27 (Copywriter)

Look @ the Store Layouts

Stores are designed to attract the customer, to entice them into a world of beautiful things, things so lovely they simply cannot leave the store without them. They are temperature-controlled and air-ventilated; damn, they should even smell nice. They are decorated for your delight using colours that score high in sales conversion and pretty pictures, decals or other graphics of products you want, products you should have. The store is also filled with mannequins, draped with clothing to produce an image of what you want to look like, whether you are mannequin-size or not. Stores are like a witch house made of candy, but no one gets thrown in the oven unless you have a serious credit problem, in which case chuck those cards in the fire NOW!

There is a science behind the method by which we shop, and the direction we walk in determines the layout of the store, in addition to the catwalk of mannequins which often open up a store or the separated walkways; the mannequins define a look for the store, which cannot be missed upon entering.

'There is a "pathway" where you see stylish, en vogue and fashion mannequins showcasing the newest, trendiest or craziest combinations in styling. E.g. Topshop in London has a pretty nice "store catwalk". The most beautiful ones I saw were at Barney's in NY and Colette in Paris. In Germany, it is not that common unfortunately.' Anna (Strategic Marketing & Performance Manager)

Look @ the Store Signs

In brick-and-mortar retail stores, graphics are synonymous with the pictorial signs above the rails or store furniture strategically placed around the store. The equivalent on a website is the home page, with style ideas and prompted articles you can scroll down. Sometimes they show the price or give a 'get the look' suggestion for a trend in that area of the store. These can use fashion jargon, to educate you on the new trend or item for the season, like 'The Jumpsuit'!

'[The brands I like are] Alexander Wang, 3.1 Philip Lim, Victoria Beckham – they make me dream. Clean, on point, so much love to detail and flow of fabric. Further brands I like and can afford: Sandro for tops, Uniqlo for basics in general, Y3 for sneakers.' Anna (Strategic Marketing & Performance Manager)

Promotions

Promotions can occur at any point in the season, when a discount is added to the recommended retail price of an item. Signs in store often advertise a promotion, as without a sign the desired uplift in sales is in jeopardy. This applies to stores and online. Discounts can be placed on a product for many reasons, including imperfect manufacturing, but without any hazards that can be caused to the customer and without a need for a label to define the issue, more like a wonky stitch and less risk of splinters on wood buttons improperly finished. Other reasons include an overbuy of the product where the sales aren't reaching their estimated forecast, and the company risks putting an increased proportion of units in the sale at the end of its lifecycle. This is a costly process for companies and can lead to the product yielding either no profit or even a loss. Promotions at a small reduced percentage often boost sales to shift stock at a minor profit cut rather than the major profit cut at the time of seasons-end reductions. Promotions are not always based on negative sales or defective products, but can also be used to boost the profile of a new product. Articles can even be retailed with a surcharge of additional profit, to later be promoted at the target (lower) margin at the new promotion price.

Sale

At the end of the season clothes go into sale; this generally happens twice a year, midway and at the end of the fashion season, when items are discounted to a greater proportion to get rid of the stock and make way for the new collection due in. Spring / Summer collections launch in or around November, believe it or not, before Christmas even, ending around the time kids go back to school in January. Autumn / Winter therefore overlaps with it, starting in the second quarter of the year (Q2). These are fashion seasons, and not to be confused with the meteorological and astronomical seasons marked by temperatures, specific weather conditions, or length of the days. Some maniacs like me mark sale dates from the previous year for our favourite stores on the calendar.

'I look after my clothes and keep things for a long time, so I guess they turn into investment items without punching out the cash. I mend clothes that have holes or dye them to get more use out of them. I think of everything I am wearing today and 80% is Topshop, as they tend to hit the marks with jersey/cardigans/underwear/jeans.' Sarah, 30 (Designer)

When a sale sign is posted, for example 'from 50%', by UK law a company must reduce at least 51% of the stock from the latest retail price to the 50% advertised. It is not a perfect science, but the signs are legally allowed to post 'up to 50% off' – a sign which lights up our heart and warms our cockles, and sends us into a frenzy, running, kicking and screaming our way into the store, waving our purses over our heads. This is of course an exaggeration, portrayed in one of my favourite movies *Confessions of a Shopaholic* (2009). The same applies for a sign with 70% off. Final reductions are as stated; the bottom price stock will be labelled up as for the current sale they're in.

You can always get a bargain if you wait for the end of season sales. However, it is always a gamble whether your size will be there on the rack waiting for you at 9 a.m. when you run into the store and not on the staff hold rail for Chantel to buy at her leisure for that gig in Shoreditch.

Sale Shopping

When shopping in the sale section, look for imperfections, holes, makeup, and dirt. Sometimes the trigger-happy assistant gets ink on clothes when marking the sale price on the label. Consider which brand you are shopping from, to measure the amount of sacrifices you are willing to make for each purchase. A famous case is with the brand Louis Vuitton, who have made the decision to never go on sale. You can probably guess why.

The Markdown

At the end of a season, when an item is on sale in different locations, department stores, outlets, online, or the original brand stores, you'll get different prices. The original brand provides the recommended retail price (RRP), but the markdown price may fluctuate across the various companies selling the goods.

If a department store, online or otherwise, has bought the stock wholesale they have monopoly and authority to charge whatever retail price they want. If it is a concession, the brand is merely renting the square-footage in store, or virtual space online in a platform, and charging their recommendations for pricing. Weigh up the options you have and ask in store whether brands are a concession, then you can price-compare on their site or other wholesale managed websites or stores.

If you are in a department store, with a limited knowledge of brands or even fashion, the brand's tag is a good place to start by assessing the value. There are also habits you can pick up which help you ensure a quality buy. When shopping in store, touch the fabric: how does it feel against your skin? Your face? Rub it on there – feel no shame for the action. Pull on the textile a little – is there stretch? Do you permanently change the shape with the little tug, and therefore know that the item won't last beyond one wash? If the item bounces back, check the sizing – there is the temptation to buy a size smaller, but don't give in to super stretch that has the telltale signs of being too small, which could cause creasing and, in catastrophic cases, riding up of the fabric. I read that 48% of British women buy clothes too small for them, with the hope of fitting into them someday – don't become a statistic!

The Mark-Up

Some products can include a mark-up, as briefly explained earlier in the promotions sub-chapter. This can apply to many products from a brand and can occur for a variety of different reasons. In one case, a brand was guilty of selling vintage jumpers from 165-year-old international company Fruit of the Loom, who specialise in basic cotton clothing and who predominantly sell wholesale, at an escalated price of £40. This is a jumper which can be bought at a quarter of the price from a stockist; in one word, rude! This is a well-known company that rhymes with Bourbon Mouse-Critters.

When stock is sold to third parties via wholesale, the third party owns that stock and can charge whatever price they want. Taking advantage of yuppies and hipsters is something that has been happening all over the world for years: overpriced baked goods, extortionate cinema entry for fifty-year-old films, and now a re-sale of old or retro brands with a hipster mark-up, which they *will* pay.

'I am an absolute brand whore but generally stick with certain brands for certain items. Polo Ralph Lauren for a polo shirt, Levi's for Jeans, Orlebar Brown for swimming shorts. I believe brands like these who have a history and precedent for styles have it for a reason.' Michael, 28 (Fashion Merchandiser)

You can also be victim to a mark-up which is virtually invisible. It could be anything from having a collection designed by someone famous, stock being sold on more than once via agents who have their own profit-margin targets and mark-ups to maintain, or simply achieving a target profit margin for the company, therefore adding a cost into the retail value. This isn't just the fashion industry; this is every industry; the more people talk the more you will isolate the brands who you can rely on.

Recalls

When a product is deemed unfit for customers, for many reasons including unsafe elements, it will be recalled. If you hold a store or account card for the offending store, you may be notified by email or newsletter; it may also be on the website, but there should also be signs in store, often by the cashiers. Without a store account (and before the now-commonplace use of email receipts) there is no effective method of tracking down a customer who has made a purchase in-store – possibly never to return. Online purchases require an email address and sometimes an account to be created, where you may be more easily contacted in a case such as this. Big Brother is not always the bad guy.

Eco-Awareness

There are more and more retail companies who also have a label detailing the ecological provenance of where the fabric was sourced or the factory in which it was made, as well as whether the fabric has been recycled to make the garment you covet so much. This topic can make people rather uncomfortable, but it is merely a fact of life: how much you care versus how much money you are willing to part with versus your insistence on buying brand new clothes. The aim is to inform the customer and possibly to make a purchase more enticing, by promising some positive impact with the sale. I will say this as a warning: please check the label thoroughly, as "x% recycled" on a swing ticket could be referring to the paper the label was produced from and nothing to do with the garment itself. Read the fine print (which is sometimes on the back) and see if the environmental promise applies to that specific product, not to the company strategy as a whole – the latter is an advertisement, and is not informative about the item itself.

Washing or burning synthetics can release harmful chemicals into the water and air. These chemicals ultimately affect the land used to grow food or feed livestock as well the air we breathe. As a result, recycling fabrics (of all kinds) has been a trendy option for some brands over the past years in an attempt to counteract the damage and volume of CO_2 they contribute to, whether it is via their own manufacturing process, air and road freight of goods or contribution to landfills. I say 'trendy' as it can sometimes appear as if it is done more for positive press than a real inclination to preserve the world we live in (this is often called 'greenwashing'). I would argue more drastic measures could be put in place for a long-term strategy for some of the larger brands, but this may impact the growth of the company.

It would be ideal to shop only eco-friendly brands, brands which look to end-to-end sustainability, which often means everything from the production of the fabrics to the conditions of the manufacturing, including staff, all the way to the sale of the article in a particular country. The type of fabric has been covered earlier on, so I will focus on the garment production, something often not considered when you go shopping. Could conditions in the factory be so dastardly that the health of the workers is in jeopardy? Could minimum wage be used as a guideline, not a hard and fast law-abiding rule? Is abuse, sexual or otherwise, policed to protect the victims? Is there a risk of being fired if a pregnancy is declared? These are only a few of the issues which are being dealt with, and in my opinion, they are ultimately bred from an industry where more stock means more sales, and high unit targets and maximum profits are the end goal. It is driven as a result of the growth in the fast fashion sector, but influences the entire fashion industry. Sustainability should be considered all-encompassing, and focus on the start and end point of a brand's produce. The labour rights of the garment industry should be a focus for each brand and company profiting off the items produced; it is their responsibility to ensure staff are protected and treated humanely. In addition to this, the governments that also profit from the industry have an obligation to safeguard their citizens from exploitation. What we can do as consumers is to keep a look out when we are in the stores, or scroll down on the brand website home page, to see how brands are displaying their sustainability strategy and where they are in ensuring it is being fulfilled. But most of all, I would have to say moderation is queen. We can slow down. The pandemic has taught us a valuable lesson – that there is a different life than the one lived until that first lockdown. Overstock would indicate that a smaller budget or units of goods is required for the following season; that is our impact. Buying new goods less frequently ultimately reduces items manufactured, wastage (faulty and unsellable goods) at the end of the season and overstocks (unsold items). It was hard learning to pay for a plastic carrier bag in the UK (in 2015), but now in 2022 all shops of all sizes charge for one. This is one way of deterring people to use this particular product. But with low-priced fashion there is no way to reduce the speed by which we purchase it; the low prices are there to entice higher sales.

In light of all you have read above, consider whether our response should be to shop thoughtfully, with intentional behaviour and an informed approach, not only to benefit ourselves but to make sure the impact is felt in the world, now and in the future.

Look @ the Shopping Bag

Paper or plastic? There are laws in Europe that say you must pay for a plastic bag if you require it, otherwise you can provide your own. Some brands provide paper bags which are usually free during normal seasonal selling periods; this was a conscious decision to be greener than their competitors without impinging on their street credibility, or status as one of the forerunners of affordable fashion.

Surely, carrying your own shopping bags on a shopping spree takes the fun out of that walk of pride home with all your different branded bags, all different sizes, colours, and shapes. Your trophies. The Longchamp leather trimmed shopper will make the experience more palatable but is by no means a replacement. To ensure you do your part, it is always handy to BYOB (bring your own bag) and reduce stress at the tills. When it comes to those plastic bags which aren't exactly helping the environment, if we as consumers reduce demand, supply will eventually follow.

Look @ the Magazines

The weekly and monthly fashion magazines are the guides to keep you up to date with what is going on in the world of fashion, sprinkled with style advice and features on different topics to keep you interested. The online version is also an alternative, but without that page-turning aspect it feels more like a blog than a magazine. Nevertheless, online or on the shelf, get inspired by what there is to wear, who's wearing it well, and what your next fashion experiment could be.

'I think stores are using discounts and markdowns to attract customers. Today's consumer is savvy and informed and needs to feel that she is getting a deal or an experience.' Shoshannah, 28 (Student)

Close to when a new season launches, there is often a feature on a relevant article of clothing. In winter, *The* coat, boot, or balaclava. In spring summer, *The* swimsuit, denim short update, or heat-tech legging. Whatever the topic, there will be a few options for you to choose from which highlight a style choice, or category available for you to buy. Inspiration from this book came when I was casually reading *Look* magazine and it featured coats, highlighting the comeback of the Crombie coat. Now, I was ecstatic about this, but when I went into COS where this coat was featured, the particularly vacant sales assistant did not know what a Crombie coat was, let alone what floor it was situated on. That made me laugh. For your reference, the brand Crombie is famed for its luxury coats, the most famous, typically wool three-quarter length overcoats. It is not a common noun as the brand has been known to sue, so this trademark word is no longer used in this way.

Magazines provide bitesize doses of fashion education for all to digest on a weekly or monthly basis. The original bloggers in hard copy are going nowhere. If you have the app, it is easier to Google a reference on your phone as you are looking at the new reason why you won't get back in the black this month on your credit card.

Look @ the Clothes
in your Wardrobe

I have mentioned it a few times throughout this guide, but I ask you to go through that wardrobe of yours and look through it with fresh eyes to create a revolution. Look at the articles you have which don't really fit right anymore (maybe they never did) and look into how they can yield a better value for their investment. If you have a wardrobe full of clothes, none of which are wearable, below are some options, depending on the cost of the article and the investment in those pieces you can't bear to part from:

- Sell them online, each item independently

- Sell them bulk to a company for a lower value than you may have received if sold individually. If the company reclaims the clothes check how and where

- Donate them to charities; spread them around or give to the charity you have researched and which gives a high share of its income to the cause

- Do a clothes swap, where you don't lose out in the end. It's difficult to have a full clear-out this way, though, especially with your very stylish friends who are about your size

- Get the clothes altered by a seamstress so they actually fit (or DIY)

- Invest in a few new pieces to bring outfits together

If clothes are beyond repair and you decide it's best to get rid of them, look into whether the fabrics can be recycled. Adding to rubbish bins contributes to landfill sites, which are responsible for reducing the quality of our health and the environment.

Conclusion

To quote the wise Jesse Pinkman of *Breaking Bad*, 'Drugs are poison for people who don't care.' If this is the case, what is clothes shopping? An empty fulfilment of fleeting enjoyment? It must be fleeting, otherwise we'd find contentment. Luckily, I didn't study psychology; I'd drive myself mad. Clothes remain a necessity if we are not to break the laws of indecent exposure, and fashion is an industry which builds and sustains economies. How we manage this industry and reflect on its impact on our environment is partly guided by individual choices, and with this guide hopefully the return rates can reduce ever so slightly. Going in knowing what you want and then matching it to what you need is a perfect recipe for a shopping trip!

This guide was written in the hope of assisting you to make informed decisions when shopping. Its original function was not only to provide transparency on the shortcuts companies take but also to make us all more knowledgeable. It has always been my opinion that in order to change the world, it takes many people moving as one. To reduce the number of plastic bags being produced, we stop asking for them. Supply and demand are the principles behind most service and product industries. Shining a light on a few industry habits may make a small difference. Enough mushy stuff – I still love fashion, and indulging in the luxuries of the industry. Fashion is for fun – to express the way you feel. Don't treat it like a chore. Take pride in the clothes you wear, and find the joy in getting ready in the morning, evening, or whenever your day begins.

Ingram Content Group UK Ltd.
Milton Keynes UK
UKHW021044080523
421365UK00007B/103